HANNO RAUTERBERG

TALKING
ARCHITECTURE

INTERVIEWS WITH ARCHITECTS

HANNO RAUTERBERG

TALKING ARCHITECTURE

INTERVIEWS WITH ARCHITECTS

PRESTEL

Munich · Berlin · London · New York

Front cover: Norman Foster (photograph by Katsumasa Tanaka);
Daniel Libeskind (photograph by Marc Lostracco)
Back cover: Thermal baths, Vals, Switzerland (photograph by
Christian Richters)

© Prestel Verlag, Munich · Berlin · London · New York 2008
© for the texts by Hanno Rauterberg, Hamburg 2008
© for the works reproduced is held by the architects and artists,
their heirs or assigns, 2008
© for the photographs, see picture credits, p. 160

Prestel Verlag
Königinstrasse 9
80539 Munich
Tel. +49 (0)89 24 29 08-300
Fax +49 (0)89 24 29 08-335

Prestel Publishing Ltd.
4 Bloomsbury Place
London WC1A 2QA
Tel. +44 (0)20 7323-5004
Fax +44 (0)20 7636-8004

Prestel Publishing
900 Broadway, Suite 603
New York, N.Y. 10003
Tel. +1 (212) 995-2720
Fax +1 (212) 995-2733

www.prestel.com

Prestel books are available worldwide. Please contact your nearest
bookseller or one of the above addresses for information concerning
your local distributor.

Library of Congress Control Number: 2008929089

British Library Cataloguing-in-Publication Data: a catalogue record
for this book is available from the British Library. The Deutsche
Bibliothek holds a record of this publication in the Deutsche
Nationalbibliografie; detailed bibliographical data can be found
under: http://dnb.ddb.de

Translated by Paul Aston, Rome
Editorial direction by Curt Holtz
Picture research by Veronika Wilhelm
Copy-edited by Danko Szabó, Gräfelfing
Cover and design by LIQUID, Augsburg
Layout by Stephan Riedlberger, Munich
Production by Simone Zeeb and Astrid Wedemeyer
Origination by kaltnermedia, Bobingen
Printed and bound by Neografia, Bratislava

ISBN 978-3-7913-4013-5

CONTENTS

DIGITAL MODERNISM
WHY ARCHITECTURE IS MORE POPULAR THAN EVER

Nothing was too high or too daring for them. They wanted to drain the Mediterranean to reunite Europe and Africa. They designed flying cities, wanted to cover the Alps with fancy glass structures and build terrace houses on Mars. They believed in the power of utopia, and that their architecture would change the world. Their heroic glass towers, odd conch- and mushroom-shaped houses and colourful UFOs would, they were convinced, bring new peace to alienated, troubled mankind. They dreamt of the "common architecture of the future" and a just, good society.

These days, the great dream of the future is over. Almost nothing is left of the idealism of early modernism and the boldness with which architects such as Wassili Luckhardt, Hans Scharoun and Bruno Taut designed a new world almost 100 years ago. There is no avant-garde any more that would dare outline an alternative to the prevailing capitalism. No one would think of proclaiming a revolution. And yet, amazingly to many people, there's more radical change in the world of architecture than ever before. The glass towers, conch houses and UFOs the visionaries once dreamt of are now being built in plenty. Maybe draining the Mediterranean will have to wait a while, but there's no shortage of spectacular museums, football stadia, opera houses and high-rise office blocks outbidding each other in daring in recent years. Many are constructed with such visible panache that they appear to be taking off for higher spheres. Others look ready for a scrap, are glossily elegant, or sublime in their grandeur. And all of them celebrate their own existence and proud otherness. It's as if the avant-garde had triumphed after all.

And what else did the early visionaries want but to mobilise the masses and win the populace over? Their hopes seem to be coming true. People flock to admire the new wonder buildings. Architecture has become the in thing. Its gleaming icons turn up in fashion and lifestyle magazines, advertising, videoclips – more or less everywhere. And the demand to actually see them at first hand is astonishing. People set off, even to places off the beaten track such as Wolfsburg or Vals, just to be able to say "I've seen Hadid" or "I had a look at Zumthor's latest."

In earlier times there were likewise famous architects whose ideas were so much in demand that they built not just in a particular city or within a specific region. They designed buildings a long way from home as well – these days they would be called signature buildings, trademarks in stone. We need only think of the Middle Ages, when French, Tuscan or Hanseatic master builders created the finest cathedrals and town halls and imposed their styles on entire provinces. Then in the early twentieth century, it was architects such as Le Corbusier, Ludwig Mies van der Rohe or Frank Lloyd Wright who travelled the globe and

Jacques Herzog & Pierre de Meuron, National Stadium, Beijing, 2008

were powerful forces in the development of the International Style. But it was not until the 1980s that architects attained the cult status of heroes and stars.

Since then, the term "star architect" has become commonplace in magazines and newspapers, which is quite astonishing. No one would think of calling Madonna a star musician or Brad Pitt a star actor. They're plain stars, needing no further qualification. Architects are not expected to have that kind of popularity, so the term "star" is used relatively, as a label to show how important and famous particular architects are in their profession – even if one's unlikely to find squealing groupies waiting in the airport lobby for Gehry, Libeskind or Koolhaas to appear. And indeed, the degree of fame such world-ranking architects achieve is well below that of Madonna or Brad Pitt, which is not least to do with their not producing DVDs, CDs or novels, nor any other product you can buy in the corner shop or on the Internet.

But that makes such architects all the more sought-after, especially among those who can afford to hire their services. They resemble artists in that their works cannot be reproduced on an industrial scale and so require a deep pocket in the purchaser. True, there are several hundred thousand architects in the world, and in theory quite a number of them could build the selfsame museums, opera houses or airports. But in the end, such buildings inevitably get allocated to the star names. The people who hire them don't just get a design but also the likelihood of global significance and a promise of exclusiveness. That's because the club of internationally known architects is indeed exclusive – quite a cosy membership, in fact, only two or three dozen architects being involved. Nearly all of them are men, and most of them come from the West, predominantly Europe.

And most of them spend their lives on aeroplanes, travelling from Beijing to Dubai or Mexico City, and the people they meet, or who want to talk to them, need either a lot of money, a lot of patience, or simply both.

It often took months – and sometimes more than a year – for me to be able to pin many of them down for an interview for the arts section of the German Die Zeit newspaper. Some of them were visibly unaccustomed to that kind of in-depth conversation, sitting back and thinking about what it is they actually do, what they hope to achieve and how convincing they find it – in short, what they are actually building for.

What do their designs add up to? Is there still such a thing as avant-garde? And can they change the world with their architecture? Those are big questions that recur in many of these interviews. The subject of what their structures achieve always came up. Were they just large sculptures, something only for the well-educated? Or is what the visionaries dreamt of at the beginning of the twentieth century actually possible? Can architects affect large numbers of people, revive cities and even become a symbol of change?

Snøhetta, Oslo Opera House, 2008

Frank Gehry, Guggenheim Museum, Bilbao, 1997

Sometimes they do become just that – in Bilbao, for example, the run-down city in northern Spain where the whole boom in spectacular buildings started in the late '90s. Of course, modernism had previously created buildings that were uncommonly popular and were made much of in the media. Oscar Niemeyer placed his dynamic power structures in the Brazilian landscape, in Sydney Jørn Utzon's Opera House became iconic of a whole continent, and in Germany Günter Behnisch and Frei Otto oaught the imagination with their gentle, playful architecture for the Olympic Park in Munich. But it was only with the silvery creature that Frank O. Gehry came up with for the Guggenheim Museum in Bilbao that architecture became a popular sport and architects a kind of saviour.

The city of Bilbao seemed finished. Everything was grey and dilapidated, the steelworks were in decline, the shipbuilders likewise. Bilbao was strong as long as the old industries were strong. But when the latter were done for, many factories had to olose, putting thousands out of work, and for a long time it looked as if they would never find work again. But then the city decided the cultural industry would take over where heavy industry had left off. And Gehry's museum building became a symbol of change, a sign of a new dawn.

Bilbao has now become the stuff of myth. Since the museum opened, more than ten million people have made the pilgrimage to the Basque Country. And even if the numbers show distinct signs of tailing off, large crowds still come to be amazed by the grandiose Baroque architecture. It is not just Gehry they gaze at: they are as taken by the story of the city and how, with a new museum and a few other architectural projects, it started a revival, boosting the economy and creating 5,000 new jobs. Not the least astonishing thing is that in visiting Bilbao the tourists themselves are part of the success story. Since then, many cities in many countries have tried to repeat the recipe for success. Gulf emirate Abu Dhabi hopes to replicate the Bilbao Effect on a grand scale, and is planning not just a Guggenheim – again by Gehry – but also a museum by Hadid, one by Tadao Ando, one by Jean Nouvel and one by Norman Foster. Large-scale plans of this kind have certainly made it clear that architecture

Abu Dhabi with the future buildings by Frank Gehry, Jean Nouvel, Zaha Hadid and Tadao Ando

is now an engine of change, a promise of good things to come. That, too, is reminiscent of the 1920s.

Undoubtedly the differences between this and the avant-garde of yore are huge. The spectacular schemes of that time were intended to be much more than a form of economic stimulus. They were intended to promote not a city or a company, but the idea of a new society. That is why many critics look on the new sensation-creating buildings as downright betrayal. For them, a "star architect" is one who produces nothing but vanities, hollow façades with nothing behind them. For such an architect, values are all about show. Image – and ultimately the suitability to act as a kind of advertising brochure – is all that matters. Whether the building is also fit for the purpose for which it was built is wholly secondary. Star architects revolve around themselves, and their buildings do not fit into the warp and woof of the city but remain alien bodies. It's autistic architecture, created solely to enhance the reputation of its oh so brilliant designer. And as for uniqueness, the star architect churns out his freaks by the dozen, dumping them down all over the world, regardless of the setting. Not infrequently, the critics get really worked up about it.

Nor are they wrong in many respects. There are architects who get carried away by beautiful shapes and design away in a world of their own, wholly devoted to their own genius. But presumably they are as common among the non-stars as among the stars. And often the cliché is just that: a cliché. Whether it's Eisenman, Libeskind, Balmond or Zumthor, the stars are all motivated by pleasure in risk, a delight in one-offs and otherness, even contradiction. But they are all aware of the constraints on what they can do, their dependence on powerful clients and the limitations of technology, and they do not see architecture as a higher form of egomania. On the contrary: it is not about their own selves, but the self of others. They hope that as many people as possible will allow themselves to be captivated by architecture and feel enriched by the three-dimensional experience it can produce, sometimes by the atmosphere, sometimes even by the beauty.

That does not, of course, mean that architects are self-effacing and put themselves wholly at the service of objective goals and functions. When they build, they always build in something of their own personality. Though many of them, Rem Koolhaas, for example, extol mainly the logic of their designs and present them as a kind of statement of fact in masonry, in truth even the most public buildings have a private core, and there is something of the personality of the architect in everything – and that stands out in the interviews collected here. Sometimes it may represent a craving for admiration, even a certain tendency to delusions of grandeur. At least, a firm belief in one's own capabilities must form part of it if one is to belong to the architectural elite. But much more critical is how individual architects see the world and what they're looking for in it. Is it stillness and seclusion, as in Peter Zumthor's case? Is it the unconscious depths of the individual, as with Peter Eisenman? Is it the playful child within, as with Frank Gehry or Günter Behnisch? Is it a matter of higher, eternal principles, as with O. M. Ungers? Or is it pleasure in the provisional, in breaking rules and redefining what's valid, as with Rem Koolhaas?

Trying to psychologise architecture doesn't take us very far. However, it is apparent that most of the "star" architects are decidedly non-conformist. Many of them are of the 1968 generation and became adults in an age of revolt. Not infrequently, their designs were so radical and so unrealistic that they could build their buildings only on paper, or not at all. For a long time it looked as if the ideas of Hadid, Libeskind, Koolhaas, Gehry and Eisenman would go down in history as fine theories and exciting drawings, because every potential client knew that getting involved with them was an adventure whose outcome could not be foreseen. Most considered the ideas of these architects abstruse

mental constructs anyway, dressed in the fashionable philosophies of the late twentieth century, with a bit of deconstructivism here, a bit of post-structuralism there.

And it is to them of all people, the architects whose designs were considered quite impracticable for technical reasons, the high-flyers, the conmen, the engineers of feelings, that the design of today's prime buildings is now entrusted. What can a cultural pessimist say to that? Just look, he would say, our society has become so sensation-hungry and celebrity-obsessed that it thinks it has to shell out huge sums erecting one grotesquery after another. Architecture is depraved, and has sold out to the global events industry.

That is certainly one way of looking at it. Another way is to be surprised, even delighted, that there is more open-mindedness than ever before, and that far more people are ready to get involved in the skewed, the unfamiliar and the experimental. And though this change is not the triumph of the early avant-garde, it is definitely a triumph for the 1968 generation. Society has become more liberal, tolerant and even art-minded. It can accept things not being mainstream, or even enthuse about them breaching the rules.

It seems to me that people have indeed changed, along with – and perhaps because of – the architecture. The early twentieth-century avant-garde imagined things quite differently, of course. They dreamt of a New Man, liberated from his alienated existence and the coercions of capitalism. Obviously, this great liberation is still some way off. Yet on a small scale, much has loosened up or been set free – and architecture embodies this loosening up. People are flexible in a new way, travel-mad and uncommonly event-hungry. They like the pace of change, being free and reachable at all times and in all places. They don't want to be tied down, whether in marriage, by religion or in a club. It's very important not to be like everyone else – even if everyone else thinks just the same.

The world of the New Man is at once smaller than ever and larger than ever. Smaller because the Internet, cheap flights and globalisation in general have shrunk distances. Larger because the flood of information is growing all the time and homogeneous societies are breaking up into numerous parts. Which is to say that the new world is both easier and less easy to take in. Both tendencies are due largely to computer technology, in that it reduces distance and enables knowledge to mushroom.

Presumably the boom in spectacular signature buildings would not have come about without this altered awareness of the world. They are a manifestation of the changes, in both a technical and social respect. One could say that they are the symbols of digital modernism. It is only thanks to new software that designing and constructing them has become possible. And they owe their success to a globalised society.

A lot of people like this society, enjoying its benefits – and yet, not infrequently, feel at a loss. They are amazed at the crazy innovations of digital modernism – and can't quite get their minds round them. Regardless of whether it's mobile phones, digital cameras or car engines, everything that was previously mechanical and comprehensible has become abstract, invisible to the eye and no longer

Rem Koolhaas, the new headquarters for Central Chinese Television, Beijing, 2008

tangible. In the past anyone could fiddle around with a car engine. These days, engines are chip-controlled and can only be repaired by computers. Similarly, in an age of microprocessors and storage disks, much has become electronic and now exists only as a black box.

In contrast, architecture does not disappear. Quite the contrary: the popular sculptural-type buildings stress their physicality. Thus two of the present day's requirements converge in them that would otherwise be excluded. One is that they satisfy the demand for virtualisation and progress. All great structures of the present are born of the spirit of computers and a fascination with advanced thinking. They are the result of simulation, and approach the extreme limits of what computers can currently do. Without the aid of computers, certain shapes could not even be conceived, and it would be impossible to calculate the statics involved.

On the other hand, these buildings also coincide with a demand for solidity and permanence. The architecture translates the desensualised microworld into a macroworld that can be physically experienced. Nowhere else is simulation capable of becoming reality so impressively – and this is not the least important reason for the uncommon popularity of sculptural architecture. Where digital technology is otherwise always interested in acceleration, where it's transitory and would really like to surpass itself, where even storage media such as CDs scarcely survive more than 30 years, in architecture it acquires an astonishing form of permanence. Seen in that way, architecture benefits from the digitalisation of the world more than just technically. It benefits above all from computers having changed our awareness of space and time.

Many sociologists even think that real spaces – the real cities we have known hither-to – would become redundant in digital modernism. In a world full of data transmission and chat rooms, there would be no further need for old-fashioned things like streets and squares. People are becoming increasingly mobile, so the large objects of architecture only get in the way. It is no longer a matter of where you are, they say – whether you're in New York or Timbuktu – the main thing is to have a mobile phone and Internet connection to hand. The importance of place has been overcome, and along with it, the importance of space as well, runs the prognosis.

But that is only part of the truth, because the stronger the centrifugal forces in society, and the more people are on the move and feel uprooted, the greater is the need for feed-back – and likewise the need for buildings which flag the significance of individual places larger than life and make the element of three-dimensionality a powerful experience. Ever since we lost the feeling for real space, and New York and Timbuktu have really seemed like neighbours, the more it seems to many people as if individual cities have become increasingly similar, full of the same boutiques and stores, with the same interchangeable façades. And the greater the demand becomes for authenticity and uniqueness – in short, architecture that stands out from the uniformity.

Architecture thus embodies globalisation in different ways. It is created by architects and clients acting on a global scale and is targeted at a globally mobile public. At the same time, it offers a kind of antidote to globalisation, because much that digital modernism undermines finds solid form in it. This architecture reflects a society that elevates individu-alism to a level of fetish. Nothing is more important than distinctiveness, everyone must have a singular personality, and that appears to apply to both people and buildings. But not only individualism is symbolised in the new digital architecture. At least as present is the desire for agreement and shared experience. And that is just what these buildings are determined should happen: they aim to create a common experience that is recognised by everyone. They want to be visited by as many people as possible. They aim to impose a collective identity and become emblems that go beyond their immediate function. In the end, individual awareness and communal awareness seem in a strange way to reinforce each other.

So anyone who thinks these buildings are just three-dimensional transfers produced for the icon-collecting albums of fastidious cultural tourists fails to recognise the astonishing dialectic that is inherent in most of them. Digital architectural modernism is so successful only because many losses are annulled and at the same time many fears put to rest. Of course, architecture of this kind cannot be elevated into a general principle. If every little office building, swimming pool and factory desperately attempts to be unique, cities will become curio shows. A breach of the rules can be positive only as long as there are still rules to observe.

But for most "star" architects, it's not simply a question of designing buildings that are formally and functionally conspicuous at any price. Often what interests them much more than the formal aspects is how architecture can structure life differently and better, or what amended ground plans can be thought up for a changed world. What are we building for? That is not just a technical and aesthetic question, it's also a social one.

How much this question preoccupies many architects can be discerned throughout this book. Most are not happy with the status quo. They still hope to be able to shape, develop and influence things with their buildings. But in doing so, they are much less gung-ho than the avant-garde of yore, and no longer project the image of white knights riding to the rescue. But many of them nonetheless nurture an idealistic urge. They believe the world can be changed. All it needs is for the world itself to believe the same.

TALKING ARCHITECTURE
THE INTERVIEWS

CECIL BALMOND

ALL CULTURES OF THE WORLD FOLLOW
THE PRINCIPLE OF NUMBERS

Without him, many of the best architects of our time would be fumbling for a hold. They need his advice, his ideas, his curiosity, and not least his profound confidence that there is nothing that cannot be solved. Like Rem Koolhaas or Daniel Libeskind, with both of whom he has completed many joint projects, Cecil Balmond travels a great deal; and yet he is not infected by their hectic pace. Even when we meet in his office in London, he is the essence of tranquillity. He cheerfully talks a lot about his many lives: born in 1943, he first lived in Sri Lanka, but then moved with his family to Nigeria, subsequently going on to study in England, where he became a structural engineer and within a short time one of the leading minds at Arup. Yet it is physics alone that interests him; though that includes metaphysics as well. The classic roles are not for him, he likes to explore the interstices. That is where he finds the freedoms that attract him. And also the projects that spur him on to new ideas and structures. His favourite project? He waxes lyrical about the World Fair in Lisbon, and about the Siza pavilion and its magnificent roof. And then he enthuses about the bridge he recently built in Portugal. And that there, nobody wanted to know what he actually was. Architect? Structural engineer? Designer?
A free spirit, that's what he is.

Mr Balmond, what do you like best about architecture?
Best? Paper, I love paper. A nice thick pile of it and a pencil, and I'm content *(he plucks at a few sheets lying on the desk)*. You see, on a sheet of paper like this I can do everything, I can doodle on it, design something, compose, write – anything, really.

Do calculations as well?
Why calculations?

Doesn't a structural engineer have to do calculations?
Well, then presumably I'm not a structural engineer. I don't really know what I actually am. But to be honest, I enjoy that. I don't have to sit down at the computer at nine every morning to think up new joint designs or things like that. I can play with my piece of paper here. I can also listen to what's going on inside me, I can rely on my intuition and my feelings.

Are you an emotional engineer?
(laughs) Well, you could say that. But, of course, it's always about architecture, only not in the usual sense. You see, many structural engineers are interested mainly in structures, it's a kind of addiction to extreme records, the thinnest, tallest, lightest and longest, and no one seems to wonder what it's all actually good for.

What is it good for?
Until twenty years ago, I was one of them, too. I saw technical expertise as an end in itself. I thought that all problems could be solved in the end if only you worked at them avidly enough and developed things and stuck to the path of progress. It was like searching for an ultimate truth. Like physicists, for example, who thought in the near future they'd understand all the laws and circuits in the world – in the universe, in fact. Big mistake.

In what way?
Just look at what's being discussed in physics today, indeterminacy, chaos theory and complexity theory, for example. They've long since waved goodbye to the old fantasies of omnipotence. Unfortunately that hasn't got through to quite a lot of structural engineers yet. They still follow nineteenth-century logic.

Who are you thinking of?
Almost all representations of hi-tech architecture are machine determinate configurations, essentially crane typologies of mast and cable, beams and outriggers. It suggests overt solutions for every problem – that's the message of architecture like that. It aims at just one thing: work efficiency.

What's wrong with that? A lot of clients would be delighted if the architect had thought a little more about functionality.
(laughs) It shouldn't rain through the roof, you're right there. Nor do I condemn hi-tech architecture, I've been involved in buildings like that. I can likewise get excited about

technical Minimalism, for example, the building like the one Philip Johnson built in New Canaan, just glass and steel, nothing else, wonderfully light and open. But what comes next, how does it go on? Do we build even more boxes of that kind, even lighter, even more open ones? I think that leads to a cul-de-sac. Architecture can be so diverse, it's so rich in possibilities, we shouldn't deprive ourselves of that wealth.

But even functionalist architecture can be rich and varied.
I'd have to contradict you there. As a rule, it defines a purpose, and is proud to serve that purpose. I find that too linear an approach, which is why I prefer to interrogate maybe more ambiguous form, non-linear and complex.

The Pedro and Inês footbridge, Coimbra, 2007

For example?

For example, I recently designed a footbridge in Portugal. Now, you might think the point of a bridge is to get you from A to B as quickly as possible. And, in fact, many bridges are built so everyone feels a need to rush across. But there are actually many other things you can do on a bridge: you can linger on it, you can keep a lookout on it, you can chat on it. So I built my bridge to be functional, to get across, but slowly – it zigzags. It's not just one-dimensional but multi-dimensional. You see, this bridge is an invitation to discover it for yourself.

And exactly what is there to discover there?

That, of course, can't be predicted. In the end, you can't control outcomes, only allow interpretations, you can leave room for them. And that's just the point: I'm interested in open-ended architecture where things aren't all totally predetermined, where there are zones of indifference, even destabilisation. So it's not just about positive feelings. Sometimes it entails distress and gloom as well.

Don't we have enough of those already?

The point is not unsettling people per se, but developing an involvement. And we develop if we are involved in things we're not used to and try to imagine the world differently and in a new way. I realise, of course, there are people like Prince Charles who vote for past models. They want everything to stay the way it once was, so nothing changes. But that's simply naïve.

Why? If you look at the towns and villages of the twenty-first century, you can hardly help but have misgivings about present-day architecture.

I'm not saying that we should applaud the status quo and carry on as we are. But we're not living in the eighteenth century any more, we feel differently, we think differently, our values are different. There's no going back, you see.

But now you're advocating the progressive thinking you just criticised.

Well now, linear progressive thinking I do reject, straight ahead is not the way to go. But I still believe that we develop, spirally, weave webs, whatever. That's how it is with the human brain. If it's not fed new things, it shrivels. So if we don't want to go backwards, we have to go on developing.

The architect as a development aid worker?

In a manner of speaking, yes. If I'm working on a project, I always try to shape it as an open process. Nothing is worse than thinking in prefabricated modules. I don't want to know in advance what's supposed to come out at the end, I want to surprise myself. That's why I try to get at a project via structures, patterns and moods. And there we are again, back with feelings. A building must, of course, be efficient and do its job. But I'm just as interested in the question of what people feel in the architecture, how the building appeals to them, what it does for them.

Isn't that obvious?
You'd think so. But architects and structural engineers don't like talking about feelings because they can't be calculated, i.e., can't be represented in figures. They'd rather hide behind functions than trust their intuition, because that takes a bit of courage. That's something I had to learn for myself. In the case of the Stuttgart Staatsgalerie, for example, by James Stirling, we initially planned the space for temporary exhibitions to be totally clear of supports, a big, wide roof and nothing else. But just as I'm gearing up to do some major structural gymnastics, it suddenly occurs to me, why do all that? Wouldn't it be nice to have a few columns here? Not because they're absolutely necessary but because they give the room a structure, because they create atmosphere, because they establish a three-dimensional quality. And I've tried to stick to that principle ever since. I don't want to undress architecture, I want to enrich it and add new layers to it. Basically like in a Gothic cathedral, where the ornament and the structure form an alliance.

Perhaps you're a closet Prince Charles after all.
How do you mean?

He detests standardised architecture and argues for architecture with atmosphere and soul – just as you do, don't you?
I think traditionalists want more cosiness, more peace and quiet, safety in past classical solutions.

And you don't want that?
No. Inspired, yes. This is surprise in new ways. It's fine by me if architecture is sometimes abrasive, sombre, or even frightening, for all I mind.

Frightening?
Yes, as has often been the case in the history of architecture and the new is often seen as ugly, because it does not conform. Just think of St Paul's here in London, that huge church. When the building was built 350 years or so ago, most people were horrified. They thought the dome was pure horror, so alien, and not a spire. The church is still an alien body in the urban landscape, but it's loved now just for that reason. And that's how it is with many landmark projects, they break the mould. We get to like their strangeness in the end, we're pleased they can't be pigeon-holed.

St Paul's as a model of good architecture?
(laughs) No, that would be nonsense, of course. Nor does each and every building have to stand out. Even so, I'd stick to that – good architecture never just follows a principle but offers us a great variety of quite different atmospheres. A building can have its light and its dark sides, it can oppress us and uplift us. And the more diverse it is, the better.

So the principle is variety.
Exactly.

Why do you find that so important?
Because a life without variety, without excitement and ambivalences would be terribly flat. I firmly believe in the activating power of architecture.

Your office, however, is located in an office block that couldn't be more ordinary – and yet you can work creatively here.
Even a lacklustre building can fulfil its purpose, unquestionably. But perhaps I'd certainly be more productive and would have better ideas if the architecture were different, if it appealed to my senses and stimulated my mind more.

Can architecture do that?
Yes, it can. Just think of the power of music, which can inspire us, brighten our mood and spur us on. For example, I like working to Bach, his cello suites, simply terrific. And good architecture can achieve the same.

Shouldn't you move pretty quickly, then?
But where to? You'd have to tear half of London down and rebuild it, but unfortunately I don't have the money for that. *(laughs)* In my private life I can't afford land here either, so I don't live in the house I'd like but conventionally in an old building. I'm glad if I can plan a building here and there occasionally that tallies with my ideas, a pavilion for the Serpentine Gallery, for example. A few years ago, Toyo Ito and I developed a summer pavilion design there that fascinated huge numbers of people. They wouldn't go away, they liked it so much. It was a structure such as never was, it was different.

Haven't we long had too much in the way of things that are different? More or less every hotel, every store, every office block wants to be unique these days, and urban integrity gets lost with all the uniqueness.
If you're talking about all the attempts at sensationalism, you're right. There are, indeed, too many buildings of that kind, which hide their ordinariness behind tilting glitzy façades. Thanks to computers it's getting easier and easier to build completely crazy shapes. But it's not that kind of show architecture I'm thinking of. What interests me is how life changes if the rooms where the life is lived in can affect you, their link within an organisational system. For example, I'd love to build a hospital some day. The shape or external appearance that came out of it wouldn't matter to start with. What I'd like to explore is how a hospital works, the rules it has and how these rules could be adapted and improved by different spatial structures. I like doing things like that, with friends I collaborate with: Rem, Daniel or Toyo.

You mean Rem Koolhaas, Daniel Libeskind and Toyo Ito.
Yes, I'm indebted to them for lots of suggestions; we've stimulated and queried things with each other many a time. I've worked with Koolhaas for more than 20 years, it's a thoroughly osmotic relationship and inspiring.

Toyo Ito with Cecil Balmond, Serpentine Gallery Pavilion, London, 2002

Many of the buildings that you worked on with these architects are strikingly reminiscent of avant-garde designs, for example, by Mendelsohn, Taut and Finsterlin. The difference being, of course, that at that time, in the 1920s, many people thought they would be constructing a new world with the new buildings.

I still believe that.

Seriously?

OK, I know it's a bold thing to say. Nor is it meant at all as heroically as it may sound. But my assumption would be that, if we're planning a new building, we must be clear about how we live now and how we actually want to live in future. What is our relationship to the world, how do we want to shape it? For example, how can we learn through architecture, handle complexity and ambivalence? The moment we ask those questions, the world is already beginning to change.

Where do you get the optimism?

Ah well, I've already experienced a lot of changes in my lifetime, and painful though many of them were, too, I was better off for most of them. As a child, I grew up in Sri Lanka, in quite a different culture from the one I live in today. Then later we had to move to Nigeria, which was a change of worlds. Then I came and studied in England, and was, at first, thrilled by the ideals of the West, its rationalism.

But the enthusiasm didn't last long.

No, it did, I still get excited by clarity and rigour. That's why I like Bach and his logic and lucid structures. But I like him just as much for what I'd call the magic. There's also always something about his music you can't explain, something that attracts you without your knowing why. The rational and irrational sides constitute a partnership in him, and I'd want something similar to be true of my designs.

You mean, West and East would meet in your buildings?

That's how I'd see it, yes. I had to rediscover my Asian roots, which took a while. But nowadays I see it as a strength not to be fixated on a clear identity but to be able to admit many different facets. It's much the same with Rem, by the way, he's kind of Asian as well.

Because he spent his childhood in Indonesia?

Yes, for both of us, that's a great storehouse we can draw on. We're not afraid of what's complex or provisional, a world that's changing. We don't live with the feeling of having to establish permanent order with our buildings.

And yet you've always stuck to numbers. You've never made the leap from structural engineer to architect.

You underestimate numbers. Numbers have clarity, but they have a magic of their own as well.

How do you mean?

Take the example of prime numbers. They have magic in that not everything can be known or understood. I find it amazing that all cultures of the world, however strange they are, follow the principle of numbers. Everyone agrees about numbers. So why shouldn't I be keen to hold on to that kind of universalism?

Are the worlds of numbers and feelings opposites for you?

I believe that numbers allow me freedom, and this freedom enables me to listen to my feelings. The thing is, architects are often in the public eye. They have to advertise, they're criticised, they draw attention to themselves. Many of them are super-salesmen of their own ideas. But as a structural engineer, I enjoy the privilege of working more in the background. And I'm so well versed in abstract thinking that I can ask fundamental questions and look at things that don't fit in the superficial world of the commercial side. That's the only way you can get the kind of excitement a good design needs. Part of it is pleasure in theory, in abstraction, but also a readiness to try out the theory in practice.

What does that mean specifically?

Well, it can be something very simple. For example, I sometimes bring my guitar with me to the office, play a little flamenco and give colleagues lessons. You wouldn't believe what goes on in a structural engineer's office.

nish Kapoor with Cecil Balmond, Marsyas, in the Tate Modern, London, 2002

GÜNTER BEHNISCH

ARCHITECTURE SHOWS UP THE WAY
WE DEAL WITH OURSELVES AND THE WORLD

Age is causing him problems, he has to use a stick, and speech comes with some difficulty. But his eyes are bright and alert, and sometimes sparkle craftily. We meet in his loft – he has had his office here in an old, half-timbered house for ages, somewhere in Stuttgart's leafy suburbs. From here he directed some of the most important construction projects in the Federal Republic. Many of his employees saw him as a stubborn, ruthless general. Almost as if there were still something military about him. Born in Dresden in 1922, Behnisch was a U-boat commander, became a British prisoner of war, and was therefore a late starter as an architectural student in Stuttgart. But the demobbed Behnisch always had a spark: he played with architecture and wanted to invest it with the maximum possible grace. The Olympic facilities in Munich, and the Assembly Hall of the federal parliament in Bonn, are by him and his team. And as reticent as Behnisch is, he cannot conceal his pride in these. But he loves even more the many schools he has built in his life. Where he always hoped they could provide children with a little of the freedom that life so long begrudged him.

Mr Behnisch, if you were 20 again, would you still become an architect?
Probably nothing better would come to mind. But you know, my grandchildren are all becoming architects, and that does worry me. I've flogged myself to death and physically I'm now rather falling apart. So to think of my descendants having such gruelling lives is a frightful thought. There must be something easier – journalism, maybe. (*smiles*)

What was it you found so strenuous?
Just think of Munich and the Olympic Stadium, or the Assembly Hall in Bonn. It's horrendous, the amount of effort we put into that. And to do it in such a way that the effort didn't turn into brute force – so it looked easy. In fact, that was the trick – to build something unforced under great constraints.

And how did you pull it off?
You have to keep the problems out of the office so that staff can work in a relaxed situation. In Bonn for example, we had an absolutely ghastly chief planning official. We detailed a partner to him, specially to keep him busy. He went to see him every week and said, "Your memos are all wrong," and threw everything back at him, just to keep him busy the rest of the week.

That got him off your backs, did it?
Our buildings do need freedom. We don't work towards an objective but wait and see what turns up meantime. We go out on site a lot, and sometimes we notice there that something's missing. And then we change our plans. In the end we're often surprised what comes out of it.

Do you mean you simply let things run?
It's probably not quite like that. But I don't think you can or should control everything. Otherwise in the end, what you get is a kind of usher's architecture, where everything is predetermined. No, in my buildings contradictions are tolerated, my buildings don't necessarily want to be right. They are open to many things, even changes within them.

Maybe what you've been building all your life is landscapes rather than buildings.
Could be. After all, I come from the country, and grew up in a small village called Lockwitz, near Dresden. After the war I came to Stuttgart, and liked the hills and trees here just as much. It's cosier here, but the atmosphere's much the same. So anyway, the fact that I grew up in the country left me with definite ideas. For example, that you don't have to surround a place with walls and hedge it in. There's a tree there, a river flowing somewhere, a hedgehog snuffling around ... that's more my kind of world. And that's how our buildings look, too, hedgehogs snuffling all over the place.

How do you mean?
I think it's important for things in the landscape to talk to each other – streams and hillsides, hillsides and fields. It's the same in our architecture. Things talk to each other, and I don't expect them to stand to attention the way I say.

You talk of things as though they were people.
That's how I think of them. Certainly there's a desire to attribute character to things and see them as individuals. That's because I see freedom as residing in a diversity of materials and shapes, in what seems unordered – a freedom in which things and beings can sort themselves out. If you find piece of perforated plate or some other component that's been retired from practical life or manhandled, it's nice to treat it properly.

Where did you get this liking for imperfections and unfinished things?
People aren't perfect, why should architecture be? I simply like things that are un-finished. It's the same with literature – if someone tells you everything, the fun goes out of it. If there are gaps, your imagination can get to work. That's quite different from what people think of as Prussian architecture. That's why there was such a fight

The Olympic compound, Munich, 1972

about the new building for the Academy of Arts in Berlin. The city wanted all the buildings there on Pariser Platz to be the same height and, as much as possible, the same design. That's order being imposed from above, whereas the order we're thinking of comes from below and trusts in the tenacity of things. And in people, too, of course.

But what's so bad about fitting in architecturally into an urban scheme?
I think individualism is always more important than great tidiness.

But not every building can be a stand-alone.
In Berlin, it was about creating a new social cohesion via urban planning means. But I don't think that's on. You can't impose cohesion, because it isn't an external thing. You see, in earlier days a master craftsman would build his own house. The business was down below, the residence on top, and his pride was involved. These days there are scarcely any reasonable craftsmen any more, and when buildings are put up, it's generally to get a commercial return. And then the buildings show it, too. Architecture can't establish order when reality messes up.

That sounds very fatalistic.
No, we have to live with it. That's simply the freedom principle – that individual things can be what they are. If buildings are nevertheless just summoned up like recruits and have to stand to attention, I don't think that reflects the kind of society we want. But OK, those are no doubt reactions to our history and the Third Reich.

Do you feel the past was a major influence on you?
I didn't have a bad war. As a U-boat commander, I was much better off than all those people sitting in tanks in Russia. Going to sea was really quite a fantastic thing for a young lad. The horror was afterwards when I realised all the filthy things the Nazis had done. That's something you never ever forget, the thought that you could have been in charge of a station where Jews were being shipped out. That's something no one can get away from, whether he was there or not. At night, I often hear the engines being run in at Stuttgart airport. I always think it's night fighters I can hear.

Do these memories permeate your buildings?
I don't think so. At any rate, it was never our aim to build any kind of anti-Nazi architecture. Many people think I used so much glass in buildings because I'd been in a submarine so long. But that's nonsense. My liking for light comes from [the workers' song] "Brothers, to the Sun, to Freedom".

Are you a social democrat?
No, but my father was in the party, a very freethinking teacher. He and my mother always had a few lame ducks in tow, I can still remember that. Could be that's where my social vein comes from. At any rate, I always thought Willy Brandt and his "Dare more democracy" was very important. And I could also identify with Carlo Schmidt or later with Jürgen Habermas and his constitutional patriotism.

Buchheim Museum, Bernried, 1999

Are your buildings a kind of built discourse theory?

You can't translate theories into architecture. You only get something half-baked. We always went about our buildings very intuitively. And all the numerous partners and staff got the freedom they needed. You can't build free architecture with servants. We always had a lot of young people in the office, they made sure we never got lazy. They did two or three projects before moving on. By then they already knew too much, they knew what can go wrong and no longer had the courage to venture on something free and unusual.

Meanwhile the time for daring has passed. The social mood has changed. What's left of the philosophy of your buildings?

Well, the new violence surprises me. The things going up in Switzerland, by Mario Botta, for example, or what Hans Kollhoff is building in Berlin, that I do find risky. They want to control everything in their buildings, want to make everything rectangular, set everything in natural stone for ever. Just like Adolf, who planned his buildings so that even the ruins would last a thousand years.

Aren't you over-simplifying there?

It's not about banning building in natural stone. That would be nonsense. What disturbs me is the high-handedness and arrogance of these buildings. I don't find that very democratic.

But is there such a thing as democratic architecture anyway?

No, there isn't, but there are buildings that come out of a democratic mindset. They don't set in stone how things have to be. In the whole discussion about whether the government should move from Bonn to Berlin, it was often claimed the old Federal Republic was unfree and timid and cringing with its government buildings. The opposite is true. A lot of things were relaxed and self-confident. But what you have in Berlin is pure angst-ridden buildings. Buildings in which only the idea of safety first reigns, the avoidance of any risk. The debate about the rebuilding of the Stadtschloss is typical.

Everyone talks about innovation, but the truth is, they're so blinkered that they can only imagine what was there before and don't dare take risks.

There's a longing for the past also because in recent decades so much soulless architecture has been built.
Yes, I can also understand that longing. Harmony and symmetry do have their strengths, things are in balance then. And I can see that many old buildings are very beautiful and very good. A light, slender neoclassicism is something I can appreciate. But I can also appreciate letters written in verse, the way they often used to be. That doesn't mean I'd ever think of writing a letter like that today.

So what about many people longing for cosiness, or in lots of cases even just wanting to be safe and secure?
Because people have no inner security, they want at least to be secure outside, you mean. I'd prefer them to be more at ease with themselves. If people want cosiness, they should get a cat. I've got two cats at home, that's cosy.

You can't accept criticism of modernist architecture.
Yes, I can, I just don't like antiquarianising buildings.

What don't you like about them?
Architecture shows up the way we deal with ourselves and the world. And not just that. It shapes our view of the world. Of course, there isn't a switch that's been flipped. But what seems crazy to us at first becomes normal and familiar in due course. Perception changes, our picture of reality changes, and with it, I should hope, reality itself.

So what can your buildings change?
I don't see myself as an educationalist and I don't have much missionary zeal. I was always against ideologists. Even so, I think that something of the spirit that goes into the construction of a building remains intact and affects people. That something of the mood clings to it, and it's mood I look for.

What mood do you mean?
Baroque architecture is a good example, the famous Wieskirche in Bavaria or the Zwiefalten monastery in Swabia. You can fly there, there's such freedom. Both were built in times of radical change, when the old order was toppled. Yes, if our architecture were the kind you would want to fly around in, that would be very nice. Just to have lift-off a bit, at least.

And in the new Berlin, everything's stuck on the ground?
Axel Schultes, who built the Chancellor's Office, now there's a rum fellow. But he's overdone the formal thing there. It's become a kind of big scene, where any moment you expect the Chancellor to come down the steps with an electric guitar. Well, and then the Reichstag. OK, so Norman Foster managed at least to take the symbolism

out of the dome. It doesn't lord it any more. But inside – some of the rooms look like waiting rooms on East German Railways.

I can see you don't warm to Berlin.
It's not a subject that particularly matters to me. I'm a Saxon, and we and Austria were always fighting the Prussians – and always lost. Frederick the Great, now there was a bandit who puffed his country up. I always liked the Austrians better. They also know about *laisser faire* and let's-see-how-we-get-on.

That was always your guiding principle.
Yes, as it's turned out.

And there's no full stop there.
You know, the terrible thing about getting old is that the world you've lived in breaks up right and left. They all die. So, of course, it's nice to go on coming into the office, where there's still so much there. But there's less and less of that, too. It's tailing off. The office is gradually being run down and merged with my son's. And that's where it continues. Almost like in a Fontane story, you see.

Do you still have a wish?
I always had this yen to buy a fishing lugger. They're deep-sea wooden boats with huge diesel engines they build in Denmark, dum, dum, dum. I wanted to take one down to the Mediterranean, where I went with the U-boat. Odd, really. By the age of 17 I already knew all the ports: Genoa, Toulon, La Spezia, the Strait of Bonifacio. God, what a lovely area. For a young lad, that was something, to get out of our screwed-up Nazi Germany. And what congenial people the French were. If only there'd been no war.

orddeutsche Landesbank, Hanover, 2002

PETER EISENMAN

IT'S THE OTHERNESS, THE DIFFERENCE, THAT MATTERS TO ME

Downtown Manhattan. A rather rundown, twelve-storey office block with a tiny entrance and a lift you hesitate to enter as it seems likely to immediately get stuck. But then we ride up with him and the doors flings open, and you're immediately amid a chaos of large pasteboard models and dusty shelves sagging with periodicals, books and files. "Peter is the most important architect of the present day," his fellow architect Philip Johnson once said. "He's an architect who needs theory, just as Mies van der Rohe needed technology. We all need our crutches."
Eisenman turned his crutch into a raison d'être long ago. In 1967 (when he was just 35 and had just finished his doctorate) he set up not his own architectural firm but a school, the Institute of Architecture and Urban Studies. It became the most influential hothouse for architectural theory anywhere. This was where architecture sat down and started to take a look at itself. Only in 1980, when he was already 50, did he set up an architectural office. Large projects came his way, the Wexner Center for Visual Arts in Ohio, for example. However, he only became internationally famous with the Holocaust Memorial in Berlin. There and elsewhere Eisenman would like to lead the feeling of space and time up a garden path. He was for many years a close friend of French thinker Jacques Derrida, debating the presence of absence, discontinuity, recursivity and self resemblance. Even now, Eisenman's theoretical writings are thicker than the catalogues illustrating the buildings he has designed.

The Holocaust Memorial in Berlin is your best-known project, probably also because of the lengthy debate and great controversy it aroused. Should it have turned into that – a place of dispute?

Well, I hope there will be even more dispute and debate. If everyone had suddenly been happy and content about the Memorial, I'd have done something wrong.

You want to goad us?

Not goad, but unsettle. Perhaps the way a picture by Caspar David Friedrich can be unsettling. It's beautiful, but at the same time there's something odd about its beauty. You can lose yourself in it, and get a feeling of being alone. The Memorial can have the same effect. If you wander among the stelae, you lose your sense of direction and purpose and perhaps your certainties as well. The thing is, all that we have in our heads about the Holocaust is a jumble of photos and films. The Memorial attempts to break the power of these media images. It tries to overcome the hegemony of the visual side by going for primary physical experience and emotions.

Isn't there a danger in precisely that? That in the Memorial you feel like you're in some maze or other, or even a ghost train?

I don't think so. But I can't rule it out, either. The experience of the Memorial will be something unpredictable for everyone. That's its strength.

Wouldn't it be even stronger if it oame across as less abstract? If It offered more specific information?

It would be wrong for the horrors of the Holocaust to ossify into a recognisable symbol, something we understand and slot into place in our psyches. There's no truth to be proclaimed in that, no meaning to get across. We can't take in what happened. It renders us helpless. And we experience something of this helplessness in the Memorial.

How do you plan a thing like that? Architecture without signs, symbols and meaning?

The computer was a marvellous help there. We fed in a few basic data, and then it churned out two quite different and quite random-shaped surfaces. We put these two surfaces on top of each other and combined them with the stelae. One of the surfaces became the floor the Memorial, the other marked the upper edge of the stelae.

So when you were doing the design, you passed much of the control over to the computer. You made chance a guiding principle.

Yes, it's one possibility for escaping the traditional notions of architecture and producing something quite different. You see, it's the otherness, the difference, that matters to me.

You look for this otherness in many of your designs. You always want to disappoint all expectations and build something unnameable. You dig your buildings in, you let figures and surfaces run together, you like to disturb – do everything much as in the Memorial. One could almost think it was just a normal job for you.

And? Do you think that's inappropriate, given the subject of the Holocaust?

It certainly could be.
You believe my search for otherness is a kind of fetish. But you're wrong there. My principles may be mostly the same – I try to get away from the usual typologies and want to do away with the idea that a building should always have four walls – but all my buildings look different and generate different experiences. So for me, the Memorial is also a wholly distinctive project, even just on biographical grounds.

Because you come from a Jewish family.
Yes, and it was the Memorial that first made me really aware of my origins. In my youth, I didn't feel like a Jew, my parents were assimilated. We never went to the synagogue, and, of course, we had a Christmas tree at home at Christmas. Even so, I feel I've something of a Jewish sensibility, which was reinforced by my experience with this project.

How do you mean?
I often feel a stranger in my city and my country, as if I were living in a kind of Diaspora. I don't feel at home anywhere any more. And I like that feeling.

But where does the feeling come from, if you were not brought up as a Jew?
Oh well, there were always people around who made me aware of my origins. During the '30s, anti-Semitism was very strong in the USA, especially in the middle classes. In 1942, when I was in fourth grade, my best friend told me I couldn't visit him at home any more because I was, after all, a Jew. After that we were together in the same class for another eight years, but I never spoke to him again. I was so hurt. He never apologised. So, what can I say? Of course experiences like that influence me, even now.

You mean in your search for otherness, and difference?
At that time I wanted, of course, to be like everyone else. It was terribly embarrassing when my parents bought a '52 Studebaker with the new look by Raymond Loewy, because my friends' parents all drove Buicks. I didn't want to stand out in other ways, either. I was a nothing. At school, I gave wrong answers so no one could say I was a cunning Jew.

Even so, you did become an architect later, someone with a high profile.
Yes, but that was something of an accident. At the university I did chemistry because my father was a chemist. What I wanted myself I didn't know for ages. One day I got to know someone in a student hostel who wanted to be an architect. Up till then I hadn't even heard the word architecture. I was tremendously excited by the models and drawings, I'd always had pleasure in things like that as a boy. So I went to my parents and said, listen, I'm going to be an architect. They looked at me as if I were crazy. And my father thought that was another of my tricks. But I said, no, I'm going to be an architect. It was the first important decision of my life. From that moment on, I was a different person.

So not an accident, a stroke of luck.
Yes, architecture gave me a strong sense of self, if you like.

Although for a long time you didn't build anything but developed the theoretical and archi-tecture-organisational side. Why?
I built from the start, but a lot went wrong. When I was in the army in Korea in 1956, I had a chance to design a casino. The very day of the opening – even the general turned up – a terrible monsoon blew, and the roof collapsed. In 1959, I did a residential site for Cornell University, but found that the design had cost twice as much as expected. I left New York and went to Cambridge.

Was that escaping into architectural theory?
In England, I learnt that architecture is not only a practical art but always has a world of ideas behind it.

Holocaust Memorial, Berlin, 2005

Even so, you could have gone on building, but didn't.
Perhaps I was afraid of failure. Perhaps I felt I wasn't yet ready to build. I had first to understand what I was actually doing there.

Does theory help with designing?
Not in the least. Designing tends to be intuitive. Many ideas occur to me in the shower or elsewhere. Of course, certain theoretical considerations do come into it, but if the theory doesn't work, we chuck it out.

So your books have little to do with your buildings.
I write because when I write, I learn a lot about my work. It's just the same with teaching. I talk to my students, and suddenly a new theoretical idea pops out of me. So I don't deliberately sit down and think up something theoretical. I tend to simply let things flow. I'm what Jung called an intuitive thinker type. That distinguishes me from many other architects, Gehry, for example. I'm not a star architect.

But you're treated as one.
But I'm different, not better. Don't know why, either. At any rate, I'm different from Koolhaas, Hadid or Libeskind.

To what extent?
Well, just look around the office here. It's small and modest, with lots of books and magazines.

Do your books set you apart from your colleagues?
If Palladio hadn't written his famous books, we'd probably know nothing about him any more. If Corbusier's *Vers une architecture* didn't exist, no one would notice his little white buildings. Lots of people built things like that at the time. All great architects are great because of their books, even Mies van der Rohe had a magazine. I write so as to be part of a future culture.

To be remembered?
I think it's important to be part of history. I think it's the same as with Faust and the Devil. The Devil can give you wealth, love and power, but he can also take them away. But no one can take history from you. And writing happens to be part of this history. I think that an architect who doesn't write is not a great architect.

What does great architect mean to you?
Great architects always break with the situation as they find it. Bramante broke with Alberti, and Palladio with Bramante. Mies broke with the nineteenth century, and so on. There were always radical moments of change, moments in which something different became visible.

Isn't this idea of being radical and different out of date? These days, every ordinary high-rise office block tries to be different and unusual, and every architect wants to build icons.
Do you really think so? To me, most of what's around us looks absolutely the same and rather insipid. Perhaps one reason for that is that most buildings don't really believe in the autonomy of architecture.

Autonomy? Is architecture sculpture, then, exempt from any kind of function?
To me, architecture begins once all the functions have been fulfilled. Where it can be seen as a unique form of culture. It enables us to have experiences that neither film nor literature can supply.

What kinds of experiences do you mean?
For example, the experience of feeling lost.

But then all I need to do to feel lost is head for the enormous, draughty expanse of Alexanderplatz in Berlin. And even many neocon buildings such as those by Berlin architect Hans Kollhoff have something unsettling about them, strange though they are.
But what Kollhoff is aiming for is not otherness but turning the city back into the familiar old Berlin of the nineteenth century. Ideologically, he's not looking for strangeness, even if perhaps you do feel alien in his buildings.

So does the viewer have to know what the architect was thinking in order to be able to experience his architecture properly?
Not necessarily. But they have to take into account that architecture has a lot to do with culture. And also to do with being able to recognise fine differences. Just imagine if we all drank Pepsi all the time, we wouldn't know what makes a good wine. Of course, the first thing is, we have to develop the capacity to appreciate a wine like that and taste the difference. It's the same with architecture, it depends on a capacity to discriminate.

To me, that sounds as if architecture were something elitist, for connoisseurs.
Fortunately not everything is architecture. That would be dreadful, like eating a three-star menu every evening. You wouldn't be able to notice what was special any more. That's why I don't want to live in architecture, either. I want a normal life. The unusual only has value if there is something like ordinariness.

But many architects inflate the unusual. You too, in fact.
That relates only to a fraction of what is built. There are only very few buildings by architects such as me, and that's a good thing. Even so, buildings that stand out and are in the foreground are important, like the Brandenburg Gate or Libeskind's Jewish Museum. We're not satisfied with hearing muzak all the time. We treat ourselves to opera as a more complex kind of culture.

Except I can escape the complexity of an opera the same evening. In architecture, any kind of aesthetic experiment is there for good.
No-one is forced to employ me as an architect. And in any case, I don't believe history is much bothered about whether the people in Borromini's churches were happy.

Is architecture more important than your clients?
If an architect only fulfils the wishes of his clients, then he is definitely not a great architect. Even so, we do, of course, build compromises as well. Not all buildings are suitable for expressing something about the possibilities of architecture. And I'd be pretty stupid to turn down a 400-million-euro job. I'm not that purist. Even Shakespeare didn't write only good poems, nor Bacon paint only good paintings. There are plenty of bad buildings, even by Eisenman.

Are there jobs you would turn down in any event?
I don't like show buildings. I think the time for spectacle is over. The time for the Gehrys, Hadids and Calatravas is past. Given the terror and the monstrous TV pictures it produces, architecture can't stake everything on images any more, either. That's a competition that it won't be able to win.

So what is left to it?
We need to keep a lookout for a new synthesis. For a new spirit, a spirit that is different from the one that has dominated us for the last 400 years and ultimately led to Auschwitz, Hiroshima and now global terror. The decline of the West that the philosopher Oswald Spengler described is unfortunately very real. And even in architecture, we can't simply go on as before.

But what would be an alternative to you?
I'm very interested in Piranesi, the shadow world of his prison pictures. I'm interested in the dark side, the unconscious, and architecture that doesn't overwhelm but underwhelms. That interest has grown markedly during my twenty years of psychoanalysis. I look for forms in which the unconscious can be expressed. I don't want to repress it.

Has your architecture really changed as a result of your analysis?
Yes, earlier I used to design only white, rational, strictly geometrical buildings. When I started on analysis, I discovered below ground for my buildings as well. I wanted the present to retreat, to leave room for the absent. You know the story of Narcissus, who saw his reflection in a pond. But he doesn't see just his reflection, he looks into the depths, i.e., he looks into the unconscious. Something similar is important to me in my buildings as well, in order to understand people.

But how can you understand people if you break up, fragment and dismember your architecture?
I believe the philosophy of deconstruction is a moral obligation. I believe I'm a moral architect because through my architecture I open up man's psyche to the uncon-

Wexner Center for the Visual Arts, Columbus, Ohio, 1989

scious and repressed side. Just as Wagner did in the *Ring*, with which he opened the German soul to the unconscious. Wagner fascinates me. And perhaps the Memorial will pull off something similar to his operas. That maybe the darkness comes out so the German people can deal with the repression of the Holocaust. I believe it could be possible.

Sounds like a kind of metaphysics? That's always been so suspect to you.
Yes, that's metaphysics. Nor am I saying we entirely ignore an idea like that. I'm only saying we have to drop ordinary metaphysics to access the dark side. That is what the Memorial is trying to do – it says nothing, just as a psychoanalyst says nothing – so that we can encounter ourselves as aliens in this silence, in this sublimeness. The Memorial enables us to be able to speak about repressed things. At least, I hope it does.

In the end, is the psychologist Jung just as important as the deconstructivist Derrida?
Yes, but only in the end.

NORMAN FOSTER

ARCHITECTS OF THE WORLD,
PLEASE DON'T TAKE YOURSELVES SO SERIOUSLY

Whenever he can he likes to fly himself, be it in his private jet, or in a helicopter. Norman Foster loves flying and he must love it. He is constantly on his way to Moscow, Abu Dhabi, Beijing or to one of the many other cities in which he is planning and building his numerous projects. Born in 1935, Norman Foster has been in the business for over 40 years. He's built many records, the biggest, longest and most expensive buildings of the world, won all the important architectural prizes and awards, and even acquired a peerage – and yet his fame is still growing. He wrote architectural history with an office building in Ipswich and an airport in Stansted early on in his career. Many office buildings and airports worldwide are built according to ideas he first formulated. Foster has also chivvied ecological building along, for example with the Commerzbank Headquarters in Frankfurt and the rebuilding of the Reichstag in Berlin. But all that looks almost modest in comparison with the projects he and his firm are working on today. Gigantic high-rise buildings are in prospect, whole towns have been commissioned from him, and the Foster architectural machine seems to whirl along faster and faster. But when we finally meet in a hotel garden beside Lake Geneva, with the sky summery blue, children splashing about in the pool, all the hectic pace drops away. He looks as if he were on holiday by the sea, white trousers, white polo shirt, a pink belt and orange moccasins – even though he's just come from the office. He works a lot down here in Switzerland now. His home is here, and so is his young family.

Lord Foster, can I start with a naïve question?
Of course.

If I one day had a notion to build myself a little house in Hamburg, maybe four rooms, 140m², could I telephone you and ask your firm to do it?
(laughs) That's not naïve, that's a difficult question.

Why?
Because I have to be very diplomatic now.

Does that mean you're turning me down?
Don't get me wrong. I've nothing against small jobs. A lot of people think that in our firm we only want to build superlatives, nothing but airports, bridges and skyscrapers. But that's not true. We even design furniture and door knobs. Just have a look here *(he opens a black sketchbook)*, I need only flip through a few pages and you can see what a variety of things I deal with. Many of them are huge, others tiny.

So why not my little house in Hamburg?
We simply get very, very many enquiries. And we couldn't possibly do everything people ask us to.

Not even with your 1,200 employees?
Not even with them. So we have to choose, and mostly we choose projects that seem to us unusual, i.e., that allow us to develop and discover something new. Though I have to admit I'm keen on many commissions mainly for personal reasons. That's how it was with the New York Public Library for example.

What's your connection with that?
I didn't know, either, at first. I went to New York and talked to the director and the trustees about how they wanted to rebuild the impressive old building. I heard how incredibly popular the library is and how it's still urgently needed even in our digital age because it gives so many people access to education and knowledge. So when I came back to London, I realized how important a public library like that had been for me once, in my youth in Manchester. Probably no other building left a mark on me as much as that library *(does a pencil drawing of the ground plan of the reading room)*.

Do you mean the architecture of the building as well?
Indirectly yes, because I grew up in a very poor, rundown part of Manchester. My parents were simple workers, and there was no one else in my environment either who'd ever have thought of going to university. I really have the library to thank that I became what I am today. It was only there I discovered architecture for myself, books about Frank Lloyd Wright, for example. I couldn't put them down.

The library was a second home.
To some extent it was. And you know what the odd thing is?

Tell me.
When we started planning the rebuild in New York, it turned out there's a much deeper connection between the libraries in Manhattan and Manchester than I thought. Both libraries owe their existence to the generosity of the same man, Andrew Carnegie. So you can see why this project is so important to me.

How did you come to be such a bookworm as a child?
(leans back) I ask myself that sometimes. You might think I was lonely, but I wasn't. More of a kind of private love affair, you'd probably have to call it. Architecture wasn't on the school syllabus, and there was no one else I could talk to about it with. And so I was really well-read without knowing it. I read Henry-Russell Hitchcock's *In the Nature of Materials*, or Le Corbusier's *Towards an Architecture*. Though perhaps read is almost the wrong word. I was absorbed in these books.

How old were you then?
14 or 15, perhaps. I left school at 16.

Inside the cupola of the Reichstag, Berlin, 1999

What about your schoolmates? Presumably they read comics.
Many did, of course. But by then my Flash Gordon was Frank Lloyd Wright.

You mean you read architectural books like science-fiction comics?
For me, they were adventure books. They opened up a world that was completely alien to me, a Utopia, if you like, a long way from Manchester. And I wanted to be a long way away. Unfortunately I didn't have the money, and I didn't get any scholarships. You wouldn't believe the things I did to get by. I worked at a baker's, I sold furniture, drove an ice cream van, and even had a job in a disco.

As a disc jockey?
(laughs) No, as a bouncer. Okay, it probably did me no harm, at any rate I developed at the time a strong desire to show everyone some day. I wanted out, and at least I got out a lot by bicycle. I found the bicycle very liberating. Even now I like cycling, as much as flying, incidentally.

And where did you go?
I biked off after my obsession, you could say. I went to look at houses, looking for beautiful buildings. I was very taken with the Daily Express building, for example, from the Thirties, wonderfully curved with black glass. But not only was it classic

architecture that interested me, I also looked closely at very simple buildings, barns and windmills. I even won a prize with a drawing of one of those windmills.

What sort of prize?
There was a silver medal of the Royal Institute of British Architects. I've rarely been as thrilled as I was about getting that prize that time, believe me. I'd just started as a student, and as every summer, we were supposed to draw a building, and so exactly that someone else could have built a copy of it just from the drawing. Okay, luckily no one ever tried to. Anyway, the normal thing to do for this exercise was to find some venerable old building, a Georgian house, something like that. I was I think the first student to challenge that. I drew buildings that didn't even count as architecture, the windmill, for example. And presumably the lecturers would have failed me if I hadn't won the prize. It was £100, which was a huge sum for me at the time.

What did you do with it?
I immediately spent it on travelling. I went to Scandinavia because I wanted to look at the social schemes there. I had a look at all the buildings by Jørn Utzon on that trip, long before he built the Opera House in Sydney. And then of course Italy. Particularly the squares appealed to me, the public spaces. I analysed them, and measured out the Campo in Siena, the main square in Verona and many others. I think my fellow students found it rather ridiculous.

Why so?
That's still the way it is. Many architects are interested in architecture and only architecture. They only have to hear the word infrastructure, and their hair stands on end. That's a job for town planners, if you please, nothing to do with them. But where would we be without infrastructure? Anyone can see for themselves. When you travelled from Hamburg to Geneva, because we agreed to meet here, what determined your impression of the city? Most probably, what it was like passing through the urban area, whether it's noisy here, or it stinks, or you feel welcome. It doesn't really depend on architecture to start with.

Are you saying architects take themselves too seriously?
Exactly *(leans towards the microphone)*. Architects of the world, can you hear me? Please don't take yourselves so seriously! *(laughs)*

Does that apply to you, too? Your architecture is not exactly known for being particularly modest.
I'm only warning against arrogance. There are many things in the world that are more important than architecture. Of course, that doesn't mean I'd say goodbye to my architectural ambitions. If, for example, I'm building the Millennium Bridge in London, then it does matter to me what it looks like and how it's constructed. But much more critical than the appearance or the construction is the fact that 7 million people a year walk across that bridge and so the two parts of the city it links are uncommonly busy. That's what I mean. That's the kind of infrastructure that concerns me.

Does that mean technology comes before design?
Why do you want to set one against the other? Technical progress was always important for architecture – it's been so since Stonehenge. And infrastructure is the skeleton
of the urban fabric, and what would a body be without a skeleton? Conversely the
skeleton of course needs flesh and skin and hair, and an attractive external appearance.
In a word: good architecture.

What would you mean by good architecture?
There are of course many answers to that, everyone has his own views. What I like
mainly is architecture that is clear, open and bright.

Could one also say cool, objective and smooth?
I know what you're getting at. There are critics who find my buildings too sober. But
I don't understand that. I like distance, transparency, I like to let the sun in – and what's
supposed to be smooth and cool about that? I also get uneasy when people start acting
as if architecture was mainly a question of aesthetics. Aesthetics are important, of
course, but they're not an end in themselves, not a value as such.

What value do they have, then?
The social dimension has always mattered to me as well. It's a matter of human architecture.

Doesn't every architect say that, regardless of what and how he builds?
That may be, but I mean it very seriously. And we've often experienced how greatly
building can change people's lives. Think of schools, for example. When pupils move
out of a dark building and into a well-designed new building, that can not only change
their behaviour, it can also lead to their performance improving.

Have you personally observed that?
There are even lots of studies about it. Now I'm not saying that architecture is something magical, a conjuring trick to transform people. It's always just a component, but
not a trivial one. A clever ground plan for example can enable new teaching methods
to be tried out. But it even often begins with the atmosphere. If there are no dark corri-
dors for someone to be chased into any more, nor other rooms that feel intimidating or
oppressive, then pupils feel much better, much freer. And that has of course effects on
learning, that's scientifically proven.

Do studies like that guide you in your designs?
In any event, we have a close look at such studies. In addition, every one of us has his
own personal experiences to add; for example, when we have to build a hospital. No
one would dispute that you get well much more quickly in a room with a nice outlook.
That's my experience anyway.

So good architecture would be architecture oriented to people's experiences.
In the twentieth century, architects wanted to reinvent mankind, and I think that was
a mistake. We don't necessarily have to reinvent either people or architecture, often it's
enough just to look at the enormous richness and diversity of buildings over the mil-
lennia. That's something I've experienced lots of times, for example when I'm out on
the road on my bike here in Engadin. In many of the villages I go through, the main
street isn't straight, often you even have to negotiate a very sharp corner, and only mir-
rors tell you whether someone's coming the other way. Tourists find that very beautiful, but there's also a very practical benefit. The wind can't whistle straight through the
village. You could say it's like feng shui, only Swiss style. And you can learn from such
models, you can copy a lot from history.

There speaks Lord Foster, the traditionalist.
(laughs) Who knows, perhaps I really am a traditionalist. I want to learn from history,
just as I want to learn from other cultures or nature, I don't know what's wrong with
that; though I wouldn't think of simply copying the shapes of the past. Why should I
do that? Earlier ages didn't do it – they always sought the right style for their time.
In any case, our needs are different today, for example we want to get around more
quickly. And the old, cramped cities were unfortunately not made for cars.

That's why the car-friendly city was invented – with the consequences we know of.
But that city has also had its day, as we're just experiencing. Of course, cars have completely changed our cities, suddenly people could live a long way out and the country-
side was spoiled by development. But cars will lose their importance – we have to get
away from oil, away from means of transport that damage the climate. And that means
consequently that our cities will change again. We're undoubtedly experiencing a
change of eras.

There is not much to see of that yet, though, is there?
No, you're right there. But the main reason for that is that here in Europe and the USA
we're very dull in our thinking. But just look at what's happening in the Middle East. In
Abu Dhabi, for example, right now we're building the first CO_2 neutral town there in
the world, Masdar, for 90,000 inhabitants. The people in charge are enormously shrewd.
They're not waiting for the oil to run out. They're beginning now to plan for a future
without oil. Just imagine, the city is supposed to be ready in 2018. That's about as if we
wanted to settle on the moon in ten years.

But the plans are ready?
No, we still don't know how we'll manage it. We have still to solve a lot of technical
problems, we need new intelligent materials, a new kind of glass for example that is
not only good insulation but also functions as a solar cell and produces energy. But the
main thing that's important with this project is to learn as much as possible from local
building tradition.

Does this tradition still exist?

A lot has already been lost, you're right. Cars rule the roost there as well, and building regulations prohibit streets from being as narrow as they used to be. But the benefits of this very dense type of building are not to be ignored. In the interior courtyards of a traditional town, temperatures are often below 50 degrees Celsius.

Not exactly pleasant.

No, no, that's very pleasant in comparison with the temperatures in the desert, where it's often 67 degrees. We have to see then how we can do it, with courtyards and wind towers and water that use natural cooling. And we have to think what alternatives we can offer to the car. That's the only way we can achieve our aims – a city that produces its own power and water, and can get by without fossil fuels.

But cars are not only a means of transport, they are above all fetish.

They can stay that way, I'm not out to abolish cars. But I've already noticed that for many people today the greatest luxury is not having to travel by car. It's a luxury to be able to reach everything on foot – the greengrocer, the doctor and the cinema, and so on. That's why locations in the inner city are often hugely in demand, in London for example in Notting Hill or Chelsea. There they are so much in demand in fact that homes are prohibitively expensive for most people, even though they'd like to live there.

And that means?

We have to rewrite the rules. In every city in the world, energy consumption is the lowest where residential density is highest. At the same time, high-density parts of the city are often so popular that many people can't afford them. So why shouldn't we build more of these high-density areas, affordable and energy-saving at once?

These areas are popular mostly because they are mature, there are many small shops and pubs, and the architecture is generally old. Can one replicate that?

That is an important aspect *(leans back and ponders at length)*. I was just thinking whether there are examples of present-day high-density city districts being well accepted. Not so easy...

And perhaps that's because larger skyscrapers make a greater impression?

Could be.

You've often built huge skyscrapers. Aren't you destroying therewith the small-scale urban structures that you actually want?

No that's not how it is. Just look at our Russia Tower in Moscow, for example. That's doing just what I talked about. The tower is actually a small city district containing everything it needs, apartments, hotels, offices, a cinema and shops and gardens. It just happens to be a vertical district. You can't build a tower like that everywhere, that's true. But in many parts of the world, high-rise buildings are the only way.

The Russia Tower, Moscow, 2005

Why's that?

Because at the moment we're going through a huge wave of urbanization that's far bigger than the nineteenth century. In China alone, over 400 new airports are due to be built in the next ten years. We have to stop housing sprawl continuing; for the sake of climate change alone we can't have our model of lots of single-family houses being copied. That's why we need high-density; we need high-rise buildings that allow people a green, people-friendly life high up. And technically it's quite possible, as we've shown in many projects – just think of the Commerzbank tower in Frankfurt. Many of our buildings save energy, and they provide a much more pleasant working and living climate. There too, our architecture has a technical dimension and a social dimension.

And a sporting dimension.

A sporting dimension?

I mean higher, bigger, wider. You've always designed buildings of extreme dimensions.

I can't deny that *(laughs)*. I like a challenge, I like the risk.

And your sporting ambitions are not exactly underdeveloped.

I took part in the Engadin ski marathon again this year. I really found that great fun. There was a strong field, but I think I did quite well. That's the advantage of living here in Switzerland, there are mountains, there's snow. Even if I want to cycle, I only have to get the bike out of the house and off I go. In London, it takes much more effort – you get into the car, travel an hour, then on your bike, then another hour back in the car.

So high-density cities don't necessarily have just advantages.

Even so, I wouldn't like to do without London. I live here and there, I travel a lot, I'm often travelling to two or three different continents in one week. I like that, I love flying. Even as a child I loved model planes.

These days you fly your own plane, you build airports, you once even said the finest piece of architecture you knew was a Boeing 747.

Oh, that was one of those surveys. Many of my colleagues were also asked, and all opted for some church or museum building or other. I couldn't resist poking fun.

But it's presumably not accidental that your architecture has taken on some aspects of aircraft aesthetics.

The romantic idea of flying won't let go of me. Planes, these bodies in space, apparently weightless, independent of everything, a system all of their own, with their own water, even their own air – that fascinates me. And then this feeling up there of a larger perspective opening up. Some of the most impressive books I know all show the Earth from the air, the view of the world changes. I like that.

And how far is that reflected in your architecture?
Mm, a difficult question. Perhaps you could say my buildings also allow a distant view, that they invite you to look around. The story of Constantin Brancusi and Marcel Duchamp comes to mind, do you know it?

No.
The two of them once went to an air show. Up to that point Brancusi, who came from Romania, had mostly done sculptures of wood, very sturdy, very earthbound. Then he saw the shiny propellers of metal gleaming in the sun, and that changed him overnight. He designed the most wonderful metal sculptures, soft and sliding, only the plinth was still very Romanian.

Brancusi, your brother in spirit?
Involuntarily, at any rate. And of course I try to design my buildings as light and floating as possible. That's why I'm also fascinated by airports like those in Hong Kong or Beijing, because architecture and flying come together there.

To take those two airports, or the giant tower in Russia, or the eco-town in Abu Dhabi – many of your clients don't come from the West. You build for undemocratic regimes. Why do you do that?
Why shouldn't I do it? Undreamed-of possibilities open up there, the thinking is radical and so are the decisions. Decisions that take ten years here take ten months at most there.

Particularly in the case of China, some of your colleagues, Daniel Libeskind, for example, have decided for moral reasons not to accept any commissions.
You know, the world is not so black and white as many would have it. Many countries that were once harsh dictatorships are currently undergoing tremendous changes, an opening-up process is going on. And I think we should encourage that process. But how can we do it if we pull down the shutters? What I dislike about the whole discussion is the arrogance of many critics here in the West. As if it hadn't taken centuries for us to develop our democracies; as if we were saints; as if there weren't breaches of human rights here too: in Guantánamo, for example. The question of morality is in reality a hugely complicated one.

Where would you draw the line then? Could you imagine designing a new mausoleum for Mao at the behest of the Chinese government?
No, I can't imagine that. But there are many jobs in the West I don't accept for moral reasons either. For example, the British Film Institute wanted us to build an archive building. But it would have involved a not inconsiderable risk of explosion because of certain chemicals, and because the site for the building bordered on some residential properties, that didn't seem a good idea to us.

eijing International Airport, terminal T3B, 2008

Is building airports also a moral issue for you?
Why should it be?

You advocate ecological building, you want to prevent climate change – so really you ought to be an enemy of airports.
I think I like flying too much for that.

But in twenty years won't all this flying about everywhere be over anyway, if the kerosene starts running out? What will happen then to all the airports?
Oh, they'll then be super sites to build the cities of the future *(laughs)*. But who knows what will happen in twenty years' time? Perhaps by then we'll have developed completely new engines or wholly different sorts of fuel.

You're still optimistic?
Of course. As an architect you have to be an optimist. Without optimism I couldn't build anything. And I hope my architecture is also architecture of optimism. That it radiates something light and uplifting.

Perhaps one could also say it's an architecture of taking off and getting away. Is there also an architecture of arrival for you?
Well, you know, I'm a globalised person, and I enjoy that. I live with my family in London, Madrid, St Moritz and here by Lake Geneva. For me there are many places I can arrive at.

And a home, do you also have that?
Oh yes, my home is here in Switzerland.

What does home mean to you?
I think home is where my books are. Also, my family live here, this is where my children go to school. Switzerland is a wonderful country, so many languages are spoken here and you can switch from one to the other just as you like. My two children have recently been talking German to each other, and of course I find that very funny, even if I understand only bits of it.

And do you have the impression that down-to-earth Switzerland is changing your architecture – a Brancusi effect in reverse, so to say.
Changing? I worked with shingles made of larch on the Chesa Futura, where we live in St Moritz, something I wouldn't have dreamt of a few years ago. So, yes, in that sense, perhaps it is.

earst Tower, New York, 2006

FRANK GEHRY

I'VE LEARNT MORE FROM PAINTERS THAN FROM SCULPTORS

We sit down in the back row, and Frank Gehry gazes proudly all around him. At the colourful seats, the warm wooden panelling, the crazy organ – it's finally ready, Disney Concert Hall in Los Angeles. Even if during our conversation the fire alarm erupts time and again because it's still being tested – nothing can spoil Gehry's good humour today. He laughs, though not for any obvious reason, and takes his baseball cap off. This building's been a long time coming, as was Gehry in getting where he is now. Born in 1929 the son of Jewish immigrants from Poland and originally called Goldberg, he opened his first office in 1962 under the name of Gehry, struck up friendships with Claes Oldenburg, Richard Serra and other artists but otherwise remained rather an outsider. So he was left no choice but to try out his dismembering and reassembling method – now so well known and popular – initially on his own house in Los Angeles, where he still lives today. He became world-famous 20 years later, at the end of the 1990s, with the Guggenheim Museum in Bilbao. These days, Gehry ranks alongside Frank Lloyd Wright and Philip Johnson as one of America's best-known architects of the twentieth century.

Mr Gehry, no architect of our day is more popular than you are. At the same time, a great deal of scepticism comes your way. Why is that?
Yeah, well, a few of my colleagues probably think that I'm a little weird, but that doesn't bother me.

Are your colleagues afraid?
They don't like it when someone goes his own way. Everything is supposed to be ultra-rational and sorted, normal, in fact. And when someone like me comes along who tends to see his buildings as multiple personalities, he gets attacked for it.

People then say your buildings are self-serving and self-important.
Anyone who says that is not looking closely enough. Being a good neighbour is always important to me. All my buildings relate to their setting, they try to set up a rapprochement rather than being just crudely dumped there. You see, I grew up with the Talmud, and even as a baby I learnt the golden rule that you should always behave the way you expect other people to. And that principle is reflected in my buildings as well.

But they're really strange neighbours, they're not exactly bent on being accommodating.
No, they're not complaisant, but they are considerate. For example, in my Düsseldorf project, I took trouble to ensure that as far as possible no other nearby buildings' views of the Rhine were blocked. I deliberately went, not for a monolithic block, but for three little towers so as to leave spaces in between for lines of sight. Even so, I find a strong, individual presence important, particularly with an art museum or concert hall. That's why I don't subject my buildings to the small-minded thinking that's so widespread in the architectural business.

What do you mean by that?
Many of my colleagues shy at doing it their own way and therefore hide behind supposedly rational things like money problems, deadlines or technical stuff. They want to objectivise every decision. But objectivity like that doesn't exist. Anyone who has to deal with shapes and materials, anyone who wants to be a designer has no higher authority to appeal to. You have to decide for yourself, trust your intuition and forge ahead.

Isn't construction much too serious and expensive a business for that?
For a long time I thought so. I had to learn the hard way to trust my intuition, my inner child. A very good friend of mine who works as a psychologist encouraged me to listen more to my inner self and not to look on architecture as the powers that be. I know that in your capital, in Berlin, many architects see it otherwise, their buildings always have to stand to attention. But fortunately you also have people like Günter Behnisch, a fantastic guy, really impressive. Pity there aren't many more buildings by him.

Disney Concert Hall, Los Angeles, CA, 2003

It's easier for you to be easy going, here in the sunshine of California.
Could be. Even so, I don't understand why many critics get so excited. Instead of condemning faceless architecture, they rant on about the peculiarity of my buildings. Obviously they prefer mass mediocrity. That seems undemocratic to me.

Undemocratic?
Yes, this levelling down is very un-American and unpatriotic. People with talent shouldn't be told off, they should be encouraged to come up with the best they can and develop something quite special. After all, pluralism is our strength, and it's a feature of my buildings. I like it if a building can be interpreted in seven million ways. But that also means it shouldn't stand there so dull and stiff like the Parthenon or any other Greek temple.

So you'd describe your own buildings as particularly democratic?
I like to imagine that they have something to do with democracy. At least they don't try to exclude. I designed the new concert hall for Los Angeles, for example, the Disney Concert Hall, so that no one need feel put off by too much pathos and grandeur. You can approach the building in many ways – via the first-level entrance or via a lot of steps that invite you to clamber over the building. Then on top there's a nice garden that's open to everyone. Architecture should create something like a community, inside as well. I've tried to get rid of hierarchies, everyone should be able to see and hear properly, even in the cheapest seats. And everyone in the audience can see and watch everyone else, they sit round the orchestra like in a vineyard so the music becomes an event shared by everyone. Places like that aren't unimportant in our democracy, which has to put up with people like George W. Bush. So if it works out OK, the concert hall can have a soothing, democratising effect.

And when you build in an Arab country, as you will be doing in Qatar, do you export this democratic model? Will the whole world finish up a Gehry world?
There's no fear of that. People will rather go on building their architectural garbage, and my handful of buildings won't change that. But anyway I'm not interested in a new dogma, I don't want to lay down how anyone should build and live. My buildings shouldn't subjugate anyone. If Albert Speer's Nazi buildings were strong, then my buildings are weak. They don't drive people into a corner, they're relaxed and allow everyone their own access. They're forgiving. Nor could I design anything else.

Why not?
It wouldn't be my nature. You see, it begins right at the drawing stage. Every time I start on a new job, I feel a terrific helplessness. I get nightmares that the project won't work. I quarrel with myself, almost like on my first job. I call that my healthy insecurity. I need that so as to take a close look and get a feel of what it's really about. If I fancied myself too much, I'd probably always build the same thing.

Yet your buildings really do closely resemble each other. There's something frail about them, even something vulnerable and provisional. Your Disney Concert Hall, for example, looks inside as if all the individual parts are put together so loosely that a giant toddler could take them apart any time and build something new with them. Everything is airy, not hermetic. I wonder why that's so.
Well, these open systems you describe come from a feeling for life. Perhaps they also stem from the fact that I've experienced a lot of insecurity in my life and often had to start over. After all, I grew up as a Jew.

Do you practise your faith?
Today, I'm an atheist, and best of all I'd like religion to be abolished worldwide, it causes nothing but havoc and wars. I go to church, to the Catholics, only for my wife's sake. But despite all my aversion I'm not free of my Jewishness, I'm still stigmatised. You belong to it all your life, you're afraid of it all your life.

What of?
Many of my ancestors who came from Poland were killed in the Holocaust. And as a
Jew, which I am and yet am not, you have this idea in your head that a new Hitler could
turn up any time and stick you in the gas chamber. Perhaps it's also because when I was
a child in Toronto I was picked on by my schoolmates; they only saw the Jew in me, the
murderer of Jesus, and jeered at me. As you see, I'm marked, and presumably my buildings are as well.

**It seems to be the same with Daniel Libeskind and Peter Eisenman. They're also of Jewish
origin, and they likewise start out with a fractured, fragmented architecture. Is there an
inner affinity?**
You'll have to ask someone else that. I have nothing to do with either of them. I only
know that I don't believe in a sane, straightforward world and can't build one either.
The inner doubts loom much too large in me for that, doubts that probably have to do
with my history as well. The Talmud even expects you to question everything. The first
word is, Why? And this "why?" has been with me all my life, in my architecture as well.
Also, even as a child I was fascinated when the Torah was read out, a ritual where the
old men used to run a silver finger along the lines on the page. And it involves not only
the written text but also the unwritten one, what's between the lines.

**There seems to me to be something of this indefiniteness, this non-explicit element in your
architecture.**
Very possibly.

**It seems to me you want your buildings to be both alien and assimilated, both apart and
belonging.**
Well, when I got into architecture, to belong was what I wanted more than anything.
What mattered to me most was power. Thanks to a teacher who had taught me pottery, I made the acquaintance of an architect called Raphael Soriano, a fabulous guy in a
black suit and black tie who always just barked instructions: "The girder goes there, put
the window here." That impressed me a lot at the time, because I was rather insecure
and unsettled and didn't in the least know what to do with myself. I came from a poor
family, so poor that sometimes meals were skipped. My parents were not much help
for guidance, they struggled along for worse rather than better. So Soriano became my
lodestar, he knew how things worked.

Yet you haven't become a commandant architect.
Fortunately, other instincts in me are more powerful. When I was a child, my mother
took us to museums and concerts a lot, though she didn't even have a high-school
diploma. And my grandmother also did a lot for me. When I was about six or seven, she
sat on the floor with me for hours on end, where we played with bits of wood and logs,
building super cities. I have a very vivid memory of that, and something of that playful-
ness still remains with me. It helps me go about my architecture with artistic freedom.

euer Zollhof, Düsseldorf, 1999

Why didn't you immediately become an artist, then?

You don't earn anything there. But I thought about it, of course. Artists were always my best friends, even now I still meet up with them a lot, Rauschenberg, Johns and Serra. I got the brush-off from architects very early on: my first building, the Danziger building in Hollywood of 1964, attracted criticism from them. In the press, it said something about broken pottery. Whereas the artists liked the building, so I always went back to them. They backed me as an outsider. And I learnt a lot from them, for example, that you can make terrific pictures even from scrap. I tried it out in architecture as well, I built myself a kind of house of scrap, a wonderful thing.

Is there any difference at all between art and architecture as far you're concerned?

Well, a sculpture doesn't need a toilet, that's one difference. But I've learnt more from painters than from sculptors. I really love painterliness, soft, deep surfaces. That sort of thing is, of course, very difficult to get away with in architecture, you can't simply let it blur, it will always be tangible and superficial. But sometimes it does work, I manage to get an effect like that with reflective and matt-finished materials.

Isn't good architecture actually notable for the art of space rather than the art of surfaces?

Yes, of course you're right. Everything begins with the spatial experience. But you have to wrap this space up, you have to get hold of it. So you can't get round the question of surfaces.

Have you tried painting yourself?

I confess I have. I simply love that existential situation: you have nothing but a canvas, your paints and a few brushes. And then you have to begin. For me, that's a kind of moment of truth. You're there in front of a huge nothing, and that can scare you witless. At any rate, after a few drinks I moseyed off without achieving anything. Even so, in my architecture I always try to get at that moment of truth.

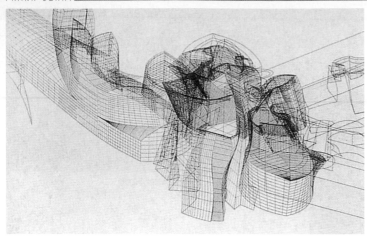

Guggenheim Museum, Bilbao, computer rendering

That means drawing and designing are much more important for you than completion.
Yes, much more important. When I'm planning a project, I always come up with new proposals and models, sometimes several hundred, to the regret of my clients. Sometimes it does get on their nerves. But I don't like it if things are signed and sealed and done with.

You mean you have an aversion to official openings?
I like them, but they are also moments of farewell. I always feel a post-natal depression coming on. But what the heck, I'm old and will soon be leaving this world anyway.

No more dream projects you'd still like to build?
I'd rather not talk about that, because if you want something too much, you tend not to get it. But an airport, that would be something. I really like planes and yachts, anything that promises movement and change. I simply love lift-off.

uggenheim Museum, Bilbao, 1997

MEINHARD VON GERKAN & VOLKWIN MARG

REVOLUTIONS IN URBAN DEVELOPMENT HAVE ALWAYS LED TO DISASTER

Few architectural firms do so well that they can build themselves their own building. And probably only one of them, Meinhard von Gerkan and Volkwin Marg's gmp, has a top-class restaurant nestling inside. As cool and rational though many of their designs may be, the two Hamburg architects know how to enjoy life. They have even planted a few vines on the slope immediately beneath their office, ensconced in splendour high over the Elbe river. From here, one might say, you can survey the wide world. No other German firm has been internationally so successful. Business is going very well in China, where they are now building a city for 800,000 people. They are known for large-scale jobs elsewhere, too — Berlin's central station is by them, as are Hamburg Airport and the new fair in Leipzig. The two of them have been working together as gmp since 1965. Von Gerkan was born in Riga in 1935, Marg in Königsberg (now Kaliningrad) in 1936. They got to know each other as students in Brunswick. They had scarcely graduated when they won their first commission, a major contract, how could it be otherwise — the construction of Tegel Airport in Berlin.

Gentlemen, is there a historical period in which you would rather have lived as architects instead of today?

MvG: We're not nostalgic. Many things about the present may not be ideal, but I don't think everything would have been better in the past.

VM: I think the difficulties loom larger today. In the early eighteenth century, society changed more slowly, and the force of tradition was still unquestioned. These days, we've lost tradition, everything you include is a deliberate choice.

Is that the reason why many people find old towns so attractive? Most people do love traditional places more than modern ones.

MvG: Quite legitimately.

Is it the same for you?

MvG: Of course it is, even if I don't like to admit it to myself. In what's called modern urban development, the ambition and the reality are almost always miles apart. As a rule, capital dominates, and that's only interested in the return. Here in Hamburg, for example, even one of the largest banks in the world is incapable of at least putting on a decent dress.

Can you think of any urban squares at all of modern times that seems to you as successful as many a square of earlier times?

VM: (pauses) Off the cuff, nothing comes to mind. But the basic problem is a deeper one anyway. We have to accept that there is a cultural gap. If urban development and architecture have conspicuous trouble in blending technical changes with received customs, the collective urban presentation is full of contradictions.

By collective urban presentation you mean the city.

VM: Yes. Think of the medieval towns of guilds and burghers. In that case, the external, built form corresponded rather closely with the technical nature of society. But the moment technology begins to change at breakneck speed, the presentation can't adapt quickly enough to keep up. Much is still designed as it used to be even though the social reality has long since moved on. We experience it as incongruity.

Does that mean architects don't follow the changes in society quickly enough?

VM: Normally, the arts, and that includes architecture, attempt to plug us in to the changed conditions emotionally. But at the moment, there's a yawning gap. All the parameters of urban development have changed, because of both cars and telephones.

But above all it's the clients who have changed. There used to be a lot of small people building for themselves, and they created the townscape they lived in. Nowadays, building is done mainly by anonymous investors.

MvG: Yes, almost exclusively. Most large companies don't feel part of an urban community. They ignore the image, the structure and the consensus of a city because all that matters to them is self-representation. But just look at the example of Lübeck: there, every building is an individual, and yet they all form a great family, all designed with

Central station, Berlin, 2007

the same vocabulary. It was only the churches that were allowed to dominate the city.
All that was completely swept away when the large stores moved in and wanted to
be more important than the churches. Many of these wolves might be dressed up as
Grandmama and architects dress them in cute little dresses, but they're just attempts to
save something by means of design. The social consensus is by then beyond rescuing,
everyone is only his own neighbour.

**But this does make our ugly cities honest cities, at least. They're quite open about their
excessive individualism.**
VM: Certainly, the silhouettes of Dallas and Houston match social reality rather closely.
What we see there is the reflection of capitalist land and property speculation and
profit-oriented companies craving admiration. And all of it without any consideration
for social welfare.

Was everything better in the past?

VM: We shouldn't make things too easy for ourselves. Take Florence, for example. What the Medicis indulged themselves with in their massive Palazzo Pitti all fell apart there. So even a free city, where everyone keeps everyone else in check, had its conflicts, for example, with aristocratic rule. These days we don't have Medicis any more, we get the European Central Bank and other things instead.

Could one say that cities suffer from what they themselves helped to create? After all, it was cities that enabled the development of individualism as we know it today. And free enterprise also started out in the cities. Both are worries today.

MvG: But why is it, of all people, the clients with the most-inflated desire for self-promotion who have the worst taste?

VM: Because they're ignorant.

Architects could remedy that with more education.

VM: A devout Marxist would always say architects are merely defined by the real balance of power in a society and can only fiddle about with the superstructure. They're not likely to change a social system on that basis.

So are you just accomplices then?

VM: We can always try to instil a little imagination and a few ideas about presentation. Those are scarce commodities politically.

But since you've now both said that successful urban development is definitely not on the cards these days, you really ought give up your jobs, shouldn't you?

MvG: That's a good question: how we square it with our consciences that we take part in a process we rubbish. Though, of course – except in China – it's only little mosaic stones we build, not cities.

But your buildings also shape the city.

MvG: Yes, that's true. And we find sometimes we also have to be able to adapt. We discovered that in Pariser Platz in Berlin, for example, where there are strict design regulations and we were planning a bank. Of course, I wondered at the time whether I ought to capitulate to the code. Then some time after that I went to the Opera Ball in Vienna, though I don't like balls, but my wife wanted to go. I didn't have a dinner jacket and had to borrow one, otherwise I wouldn't have been let in. And it's true, the Opera Ball wouldn't have been the Opera Ball unless everyone were in white ties and tails. Only that way does it have something special about it, an aura.

And how does that relate to urban development?

MvG: I mean that even in cities certain conventions have to prevail.

What about if the tails rule prescribed historicist columns or similar ornaments?

MvG: That's where I'd draw the line. After all, I can take the tails off at the end of the evening, which is not so easy with a dolled-up building.

Museum, Shanghai-Pudong, 2002

VM: Design rules should only be there to preserve a city's identity. In the demolished part of Friedrichstadt in Berlin, at least a minimum of consensus is the aim, even if all the architects are groaning about the Procrustean bed of the perforated stone facade.

Lots of places have design regulations, but they don't improve things much.
VM: Let's be specific for once. Just try to find a farmhouse in Schleswig-Holstein to celebrate a wedding, one that isn't messed up. You'll find only devastated, ruined places, whether it's Elmshorn or Itzehoe. Your eyes would pop out at the horrors of mangled buildings and farmhouses. But then you go through Upper Bavaria and find that almost every village has its design regulations – and it's a nature and architectural park, you're travelling through.

Does that mean everything has to stay the way it was?
VM: No, the regulations gradually change, but cautiously. They evolve. And cities are evolutionary in essence. Revolutions in urban development have always led to disaster.

Then why are you taking part in a revolution and building from scratch the new city of Lingang for 800,000 people near Shanghai?
VM: There's nothing to develop there. It's a tabula rasa.
MvG: I'm currently working on the design regulations. Size of plots, height of build-ings, materials – all that will all be laid down there so as to facilitate something like variety in unity. At the same time, I am aware, of course, that what we're doing there is all a bit theatrical.

Was at any time in the history of the twentieth century a new city of that size ever built successfully?

VM: We really do have to watch that we don't throw the baby out with the bathwater. In the nineteenth century, when European cities exploded just as the Chinese cities are doing now, there were endless large-scale plans. And yet we nowadays like Victorian districts.

MvG: But those are residential areas you're talking about. There are no successful models for ordinary commercial districts.

What ideals do you look to when you're designing a city?

MvG: We're trying to do a few things differently. Elsewhere it's generally the case that the most expensive land is in the city centre. This can generally be afforded only by owners who don't generate any life in the city: banks, insurance companies, office blocks, and so forth. Also, cities that are city-centre-based create the most traffic there. The truth is that the centres of many cities are, from a human point of view, a vacuum. So we're trying for the opposite, we're putting a lake in the centre that will never be filled in, putting the cultural buildings on a few islands, and all the top addresses round the shore of the lake. They're all in the same position, all looking towards the centre, which is a collective centre. The water, the shore and the promenade are inviting to the inhabitants, and to lots of visitors, too. Because there's nothing like it anywhere in China.

ingang New City, near Shanghai, model

Is today's ideal city a leisure city?

VM: No, what's it's all about is a more complex social vision, that public space should be equally used by everyone.

MvG: We're also planning, for example, that all public buildings should be detached and free-standing. No other buildings will be free-standing. And that's very radical in itself, because these days virtually everything is free-standing.

VM: At the back of our minds, Hamburg was the model, with the Alster river in the middle.

But why is the design of this Chinese Alster so strictly radial? The evolutionary cities you're keen on don't have that sort of thing.

VM: It's a cliché cluttered up with romantic ideas that a good city always has to be cosy and enchanted. Why shouldn't the grid systems of classical Greek or Spanish colonial cities also have their value? We need to stop this mystic fug of cosiness. Grids and rational ideas aren't inhuman. I say that particularly because, especially in Germany at the moment, there's a panic-stricken fear of thinking and building large-scale.

MvG: China is, for us at least, a stroke of luck. It can't be compared with Europe. It's not brick walls we run into there but a vacuum. That's wonderful, although of course we don't know whether we shall attain our main objectives. The decision makers change abruptly.

VM: Yes. You should try dancing with an empty space some time.

So really, in the end the stroke of luck could turn out a curse?

MvG: I recently got to know an Indian who looked enviously at the Chinese because they do their cities much more quickly. I asked him why that was. We're a democracy, he said. China is a centralised state that can decide where to slap down a high-speed train. It doesn't need to take notice of anyone.

So your client is a kind of absolutist client. China is your eighteenth century!

MvG: It probably wasn't such a bad time then, after all.

The Christ Pavilion, Expo, Hanover, 2000

ZAHA HADID

MY BUILDINGS PROMISE OPTIMISM

Dressed totally in black, her hair loose, her voice husky and deep, she sits there and holds court, even if this court is only the Mercer Hotel in deepest SoHo in New York City. They're all there, Roger, Sandra, Erica, Sarah, Susan, Ari, a crowd of assistants, friends, press people, all buzzing around her, and she revels in it. An interview right now, of all times? She'd prefer to do what she most likes doing – phoning around, to find out where everybody is who happens not to be there. She loves being at the centre of things – and it took so long to get there. She was despised and laughed at for her unconventional designs. Hadid is the only woman in the global architectural business, atypical also in her origin in Baghdad, where she was born in 1950. To start with, she studied mathematics – likewise rare. Later she switched to architecture, starting work with Rem Koolhaas in 1977. Three years later she opened her own office in London, initially without much success. Nobody seemed to want to build her shard-like designs. Only a few German clients screwed up enough courage: she designed a fire station for Vitra in Weil am Rhein, the Science Centre in Wolfsburg, a factory for BMW in Leipzig. Now her office is overwhelmed with major contracts: China calls, the Near East flocks to her, even in England she's getting work. Everyone wants her, and she's everywhere and nowhere, a nomad in the global construction industry.

Ms Hadid, are you a happy person?
How do you mean? Well, I like it if a lot's going on. And at the moment, there are a
whole lot of things going on.

Actually, you're always on the move.
Yes, a lot of people say it's typical Iraqi, a born nomad, but that's rubbish, of course.
That's how it is for all successful architects, you have to be on the road. After all, clients
want to see us at least once in a while. And the more clients there are, the worse it is.
I think these last weeks I've actually been on a plane all the time.

And that's what you call happy?
Travelling wears you out nicely. I used to love going to the cinema and the ballet.
I found that interweaving of bodies, space and movement immensely exciting. But I
don't get round to anything any more.

But you still get round to designing. Don't you need a bit of peace and quiet for that?
Architects can't do everything themselves. A lot of people think, yes, architecture's a
matter of inspiration, a flash of lightning that hits you, and the brilliant design is done.
But architecture is much more complicated than that, lots of people are involved, a
design like that evolves slowly. In the past, we used to do at least ten models for every
job, we wanted to know everything that was possible. I live off that today, that's my
stockpile. And I have good people I can trust with whom I'm always in contact. I can
say to them, my telephone bill ... *(checks to see if a new text message has arrived)*

Do you still design things yourself?
I don't touch computers, I never liked the things, particularly the mouse I find awful.
But presumably that's a mistake, I should have got to grips with them ten years ago. It's
crazy all the things you can do with these new programs. Well, perhaps I'll get round to
finding a teacher, but I think I'm too impatient.

Paper is more patient.
Yes, in quiet moments I still work with my sketchbook. Then I sketch away frantically,
500 sheets soon get used up.

500 sheets?
Well OK, perhaps 200. At any rate, it's an opportunity for me to run through some
ideas.

For specific projects?
No, it tends to be abstract spatial ideas that keep me busy. Questions of how the relationship of floor and wall and ceiling can be redefined. I must admit I rarely get round to
that. I moved a little while ago, into a new loft extension. A wonderful flat, but I haven't
yet warmed to it. I haven't yet settled in, I don't have time.

Vitra fire station in Weil am Rhein, 1993

At the moment, you're getting a lot of big jobs. The number of your staff has more than doubled, from 60 to more than 150 in a short time.

150? Yes, could be, roughly. If you want to know exactly, you'll have to ask Patrik.

Your business partner Patrik Schumacher.

Yes, he takes new people on every day, though I find it's really getting to be too many people, but probably there's no other way.

How come the sudden success?

Well, I've been able to do some things in your country, in Germany, the fire station in Weil and the Phaeno Science Center in Wolfsburg. The Germans take a chance, perhaps more than they sometimes think. At home in England, there's virtually nothing by me, and in other places as well many people tend to laugh at me. Fantastic drawings, they say. Looks a bit crazy, as a design. But that couldn't be built. They wanted to write me off as a paper architect. I was considered eccentric.

Not wholly without justification, though? The Times called you England's best-hated architect.

Did they? *(laughs)* I don't remember that at all. Many people think I'm a volcano permanently spewing fire. But I'm simply a very emotional person. I get immense pleasure

from certain things, and I can get annoyed as well – very annoyed. Most English people don't know how to handle that. Sometimes I simply screamed at them, just to faze them. But I wouldn't do anything like that any more these days, of course. *(laughs)*

Has success tamed you?
I wouldn't say that. I go on doing what I want to do. Perhaps sometimes you have to be difficult, otherwise only mediocre stuff comes out, and we have enough of that. I don't like compromise, so there's often friction.

What about, exactly?
Perhaps it's because I'm not European. The way I think is a bit different from the classic European, who looks at things rationally. Most architects are like that, what interests them is clarity and predictability. I belong to a tradition in which intuition and logic are more closely connected.

Do you see yourself as an Arab architect?
Many people say that – Rem Koolhaas, for example, with whom I collaborated for a while. But I'm not going to let myself be shoved into that kind of role. I can't wholly deny, of course, that I come from a culture that's 5,000 years old. I'm Babylonian. History is nothing I'd have to fight for. To me, history is simply a fact, and I can and should throw my ideas for tomorrow at it.

Are you rid of history?
I don't have to cling to any kind of historicism. I don't live with the feeling that history might get lost.

But doesn't your architecture also live from history?
Do you mean the calligraphy of the Arabs, which flows very freely like my buildings?

I was thinking more of the Russian avant-garde of the early twentieth century that you often refer to, Malevich or Leonidov. You adopt their ideas. Isn't that a kind of historicism?
But I don't slavishly copy their designs. What I want is to update notions they had then, to make the idea of a new order fruitful for us. That was never tried out properly. At that time, they hoped for a new start: a new architecture would arise that would throw off all constraints and call everything into question. Do houses have to stand on the ground? Can they float as well? What's a wall? What's the floor? Do we have to follow the tyranny of right angles, or can we tap into the other 359 degrees? They're still major questions today.

The avant-garde were mainly interested in a new social order. What about you?
Many of the modernist dreams have gone phut. And a lot of it was plain wrong-headed, the idea, for example, that humanity could be saved by concrete blocks. But that doesn't mean that the modernist project is done with. It just needs a new modernism to do away with old mistakes. That's why our buildings don't look the same everywhere, they try to be just right for the place and the user. And many

of them aim to redefine the relationship between private and public. We raise many of our buildings so as to leave the space beneath free for urban living. We dissolve the classic boundaries.

That sounds very stereotyped.
You can't set out a clear agenda any more. It's different from classic modernism, which knew exactly how it wanted to liberate people. These days we can only formulate ideals. I want spaces that are not closed, that have no predetermined orientation, that allow many flows and stimulate movement.

You mean, like with the sofas you've designed. They're curved and diagonal and often backless, so you can't sit on them for more than a quarter of an hour at a time – they force you to move.
You haven't developed the right sitting technique yet. *(laughs)* I want things to remain fluid, soft and busy. Not everyone needs to feel at home in them, I don't want easy answers for everyone. I want to put forward new styles of living. I don't want to pre-scribe them.

But isn't a curved wall much more impractical than a straight one? It expects more adjust-ment from residents. That's what I suspect – that your buildings have something prescrip-tive, even if they look flexible.
Are you picking a quarrel? Listen, everyone, I think he's picking a quarrel. You probably don't like my architecture.

I'm only asking whether your architecture keeps its promises.
But that's very simple. My buildings promise optimism. These days it's a bit difficult to talk of utopias, but perhaps we should do that ourselves again. I believe at any rate that something can be expressed in architecture we don't even suspect is possible – a new order of things, a different view of the world. That has a political dimension for me. When I started architecture at college in London, every idea of progress had been squashed. There were a few people who did hi-tech, people like Norman Foster, who aimed at superlatives with their designs. And there were the large group of tradition-alists, a suffocating postmodernism. At least my architecture shook that off, I think. It proved that not everything has to stay as it was forever. So that would make a nice ending for your interview. Shall we stop there?

Can I ask one more question? I'd like to know where your faith in the new comes from.
Everything changes, the way we work, technology, art. Why should everything stay the same in architecture, of all things? I don't see that. I grew up in Baghdad when a lot of things were beginning to change in Iraq. My family were very privileged and very

haeno Science Centre, Wolfsburg, 2005

Moon System Sofa, 2007

prosperous, and my parents sent me to a convent school, where Catholic nuns taught us. One thing they got across more than anything – to believe in ourselves. It was taken for granted that girls could also achieve something, and they, too, could be good at scientific subjects. Almost all of us have done something with our lives.

But you studied mathematics at first.
Yes, but only for a while. Maths came easily to me, I could do it in my sleep. So I thought, OK, let's begin with that. But I actually wanted to become an architect, I wanted that by the time I was eleven. The most wonderful new buildings were going up in Baghdad at the time, I could watch it happening every day. That was a very memorable experience. Society was changing, something new was on the way. And this new thing was proclaimed in the architecture.

Can you imagine ever going back to Baghdad?
My roots are still there, and I'd like to consider how the city could be rebuilt and reinvented. But today London is very important to me as well. At first I was the confused foreigner, non-British, and a woman moreover, and many of my colleagues found that unsettling. Since then, we've got used to one another.

So far, you're more or less the only woman among the internationally well-known architects.
People keep asking if women work differently from men. I can only say that I don't know, I've never been a man. But obviously most clients don't quite dare to get mixed up with a woman. It takes an Iraqi woman to show them how.

You even get design jobs for kitchens and cutlery. Aren't you afraid of a cliché? Many people are already talking about the design domina.
What rubbish! I think it's wonderful to design something else from time to time. We've just done a car, and I've done quite a lot of furniture. I don't want to be restricted to just one task, I want to take in the whole world. If time permits.

So far you've built only iconic buildings, no residential stuff, least of all social housing.
That's not up to me. I don't see my buildings in the least as something highly exclusive, something for the elite. Artistic self-realisation is not what it's about, I want mainstream. I'd be glad to think about how life tomorrow could be designed for the working class as well. Though the regulations in social housing design are so incredibly strict that scarcely anything can be changed. That's a shame. Modernism came up with a lot

of terrific innovations particularly in residential buildings. As a German you know that better than anyone. Is anything happening back home in that respect?

Social housing construction is as good as dead.
Remarkable that so little should be coming from Germany. I'm a great admirer of Erich Mendelsohn – and Mies van der Rohe, of course. These days no Germans play in the top league any more, not much more has been heard since O. M. Ungers.

What's the explanation?
I think things have been too good for German architects. They had so much to do at home that they've almost said goodbye to the international level. There are some good firms. I very much admire Sauerbruch & Hutton, for example. But many of those who were once abroad and then returned to Germany seem to be wasting away there.

You don't have any work on in Germany at the moment.
I don't know why. Perhaps people don't need my optimism there any more.

JACQUES HERZOG & PIERRE DE MEURON

ARCHITECTURE AS ART IS INTOLERABLE

Only by a hair's breadth did they fail to come into the world as identical twins. Both were born in 1950, both in Basle, one mid-April, the other early May. They both studied at the Swiss Federal Institute of Technology in Zurich, graduated together, and jointly set up as architects in 1979. And yet they are different in many ways. One of them, Pierre de Meuron, looks more like the Home Minister, the other, Jacques Herzog, is the Foreign Minister. It's the latter I meet in the interview, in a converted garage immediately alongside the buildings that they have filled with their steadily growing team. Herzog looks rather like a marathon runner, lean and tense; the development of their office seems like a never-ending last lap. Ever since they converted an old power station in London into the Tate Modern, they have gained one major job after another, with enquiries streaming in from all over the world. And time after time, they come up with different, but amazing solutions. Their two large stadiums for Munich and Beijing could likewise be identical twins, and yet they are fundamentally different. The firm loves creating offbeat atmospheres with unusual materials. And one only rarely notices in the buildings the pressure and haste with which they came into being. Herzog jumps up before the interview is really over. He has to go and catch the next plane. Fortunately for his buildings, there is always someone left behind, his unidentical twin, Pierre de Meuron. Depart and stay put, that's their principle – indeed, the paradox that makes their architecture so vital.

Mr Herzog, what's happened exactly? Your firm has long been known for its rigorous, cool architecture – puritanical minimalism, in fact. Meantime you've come up with a Philharmonic with undulating shapes for Hamburg and a soft-structure football stadium for Munich. Asceticism has become sensualism. Have you betrayed your principles?
Not at all, we're faithful to them more than ever. When I was new to my profession, we wanted to offer an abstract, minimalist alternative to the formal exuberance of postmodernism. But then we gradually noticed that minimalism is also a trap. Purification and clarification of form has something sectarian and Protestant about it. Modernism as a whole was about getting away from ornamentation and sensuousness. It depended on the notion of subjecting everything to the same grid. It drove out irrationalism and localism.

And that's why you're converted?
What makes you think that?

In many of the exhibitions about your firm, you show, for example, purely fairy-tale objects that bear only a remote resemblance to architectural models. Lots of tinkering, modelling, playing around – as if architecture were the high art of the unconscious.
It probably is that, but by no means exclusively so. What we want to relativise is not the rational side but the ideological side of modernism. Our means to that end have always been much more of a conceptual and intellectual nature than craftwork. So what you call fairy-tale is in truth also driven by clear thinking. The red sugar, for example: we didn't melt any old sugar, we knew exactly how the material would behave. Though the loops and bubbles may nonetheless have something random about them, it's a programmed randomness.

And what interests you about it?
I've always been fascinated by shapes that elude any definition. Ideally, they trigger off complex associations and cannot be interpreted unambiguously. For us, architecture is a form of thought that should offer extensive incentives for us to become aware of ourselves and the world.

But your buildings don't look in the least cerebral.
Nor should they. What's important are the unconscious impressions – everything that's communicated to you via the materials, smells and acoustics of a building. The aim with our buildings is to tone down the visual side a bit and appeal to all the human senses.

Isn't the general flood of stimuli bad enough already?
Well, OK, but generally it's the negative charms of ugly architecture you get to notice. There's nothing in that to say beautiful things can't be appealing.

You work on buildings of beauty?
Beauty is, in the end, what moves all of us most. Though I don't necessarily mean by that something harmonious and polished, but more the kind of beauty that seduces

Allianz Arena, Munich, 2006

and bewilders. For example, something that gets great depth from a surface, in a Marcusean sense. Most people don't notice architecture anyway. But for all the rest, it should as far as possible be a pleasure and a surprise, and stimulate perception. We all spend too much time without being aware that we're there at all. Architecture can help to change that, and get across a quasi-Buddhist attitude to the world in which everyone is receptive to what is.

Doesn't an architect have to think more politically?

But that's eminently political, in the sense that everyone develops a more critical awareness. Furthermore, in the original meaning of the word *polis*, the political side can be developed only from the specific individual project. To take an example: we built the Edificio Forum in Barcelona, an exhibition and conference building, huge, for 3,000 people. Normally, buildings like that are accessible to only a small proportion of society – the rest remain outside. That way, the building would have become a kind of non-place, a hostile object. But because we want it to be still loved even in 20 years' time, we raised the building to leave room for a covered square with light wells and fountains beneath. We also persuaded the mayor to organise a weekly market on the site and erect a chapel. So we wanted to create a new public space that would also be accepted by people who otherwise have nothing to do with conferences and exhibitions. Admittedly, you can't generalise from this example – formulate rules and universal panaceas as modernism used to love doing. These days, architects have to rethink everything case by case.

Do a kind of punctuation job?
The architects of modernism believed in a mission – a better city for a better mankind for a better future. Today it's counted a success if they can attract and connect a bit and divert a few electricity cables. But many are content to erect a few fenced-off architectural idols.

Your Prada building in Tokyo is one of those idols as well, isn't it?
It's certainly become a kind of cult location. But I'm not saying in the least that every building must be open to all social classes, like in Barcelona. The critical thing for us is that architecture should be accepted and esteemed – loved, in fact.

And how far do you go to win that love? Would you decorate your façades with columns and a tympanum?
Not with a completely new building, at any rate. But if the point is to add something somewhere, why not?

You have nothing against reconstructions?
Reconstruction should be one of an architect's or urban developer's options today like a tabula rasa, i.e., building from scratch. For us, it's solely a matter of the place and what's got to be built. Reconstructing the Frauenkirche in Dresden, for example, seems to us the right thing to do because the liturgical content has remained the same as before the destruction. I'd also be for the rebuilding of the Twin Towers in New York, which would be a much more impressive urban development statement than the present plan with all the design drivel. That would also have had an explosive aesthetic and emotional power far surpassing any memorial.

Sounds like a very postmodernist attitude, as if everything were interchangeable and as it comes.
Everything is interchangeable and as it comes. You see, modernism aimed to establish new standards that in the end could have led to a new tradition. But because that didn't work out, we now don't have a tradition – any compulsory rules or ideological finger-wagging. That's the reason why there's so much ugliness in cities today, but at the same time it offers hitherto unparalleled opportunities for extraordinary things or new things. Today, China is the place where ugliness and extraordinary things are being built in their most extreme forms and with extreme rapidity. We're designing a new urban area for 300,000 people there and are trying to offer as many different spatial typologies as possible for urban living.

Though the twentieth century has shown that sophistication, unpredictability and multi-facetedness are totally beyond the reach of planning.
Yes. Mainly there were fallacies and bodged planning.

And you want to add another mistake to the fallacies?
The city is needed, so someone has to build it. The question is only how one does it. Because we can't give a fundamental answer to that, only a specific, tangible one, we've looked at the job as a single, large architectural project and developed it from the inside out, from everyday life in the city. Together with people on the spot and Chinese artist Ai Wei Wei.

Normally in urban development, residential and office districts are still kept strictly separate from each other. Are you ditching that paradigm of modernism as well?
There are several projects for living and working in China where we want to bring the two together – formal radicalism and programmatic mixing. That would be difficult to implement at home, even though investors in the West have recently shown themselves more receptive to hybrid uses.

But so far your firm has rarely had any part in developing new architectural approaches to styles of living and working.
Residential projects are very difficult in Switzerland. The subsidy system is very pernickety, and the established styles of living don't leave much room.

But many architects are also too comfortable to get involved in laborious jobs of that kind, particularly as there's not as much prestige in a residential building as in a museum. In that respect, classic modernism, which you're so ready to criticise, was a step or two ahead of the present day. In the twenties, radically new ground plans and residential ideas were developed, and they didn't necessarily have more money than today.
The architects of modernism took residential buildings as basic models for the design of a new, modern society. As we can now see, not much is left of this idea of a new society, which is why residential experiments only occasionally crop up. Architects' room to manoeuvre is now somewhere else, and it's constantly shifting. In the past, it was churches, now it's museums or flagship stores like our Prada store in Tokyo, for example. Projects like those are successful if the clients and the architects get together as radical conspirators.

Is it really so important to think radically? It seems to me more that cities lack well-designed middle-of-the-road buildings. Every new building tries to be something special, and the result is cities that don't hang together.
But they fail to hang together not primarily because of the buildings but because of the people. It's still always people who build cities the way they happen to be able to. That's why cities are a kind of petrified psychological landscape. These petrifactions fascinate us in all their possible manifestations, whether middle-of-the-road or well designed. That's why we've begun to look at the issue systematically, not just at the

Herzog & de Meuron office but with our students as well. And it's made us still freer in the way we see things, and less ready than ever to be bound by ideologies of any kind.

Does that explain the change in your architecture?
This change was and remains necessary for us to survive. We see architecture and urbanism as vehicles for understanding something. And perceiving a changing world. To that extent, the architectural output of any architect is naturally an image of the world, and to a much greater extent an image of itself.

But why has your architecture developed so suddenly?
For us, extending the form and content was also a strategy to escape any kind of pre-definition, including branding, while still leaving us in full view. Many artists, Thomas Ruff is one, for example, work the same way today, constantly coming up with new categories of work and pursuing them in parallel with others.

You've always liked mixing with artists. Any particular reason?
Real artists are incorruptible and honest. That may sound dumb, but it's true, because art can only be generated once all conventions, clichés and influences have been thrown overboard.

Do you feel you're an artist yourself?
Architecture, art, fashion, film and music have all moved much closer than they used to be. We can work well with artists, but also with fashion leaders such as Miuccia Prada, because our ways of working and thinking have come closer together. As I explained a while back, all firm landmarks and traditions have vanished, leaving a vacuum that architects have to fill with their own strategies and concepts, as long as they're capable of it. In that respect, architects and artists are related these days. But the product that emerges from it is quite different. Architecture is architecture, art is art. Architecture as art is intolerable!

Artists are trailblazers for you, it seems to me. In Eberswalde, for example, you built a library solely of concrete slabs with pictures by Thomas Ruff printed on them – as if he had to supply the ornament you didn't trust yourselves to do.
We were Thomas's trailblazers and he was ours. We merrily misused each other and thereby helped each other. Instead of photos on the wall, suddenly there was a whole building …

… a rigorously minimalist structure, a paragon of picturelessness which you nonetheless printed with pictures. Isn't that almost schizophrenic?
Not schizophrenic. Paradoxical maybe. There's something iconoclastic about it, and at the same time something enormously vivid. It's a weird hunk, and yet one of our most beautiful buildings.

ibrary of the Technical University in Eberswalde, 1998

PHILIP JOHNSON

ARCHITECTURE IS ART, NOTHING ELSE

*He sits right at the top, where else? And where else should he have his office than in the famous
Seagram Building built by the celebrated Ludwig Mies van der Rohe in New York? Of course,
he could also live in an office block that he designed himself. There are a number of those in
Manhattan, the Lipstick and AT&T buildings, for example. Yet Philip Johnson likes a degree of
understatement. He doesn't need to have designed the whole building. It's enough if some people
know that he took part in the design for the Seagram. Johnson is a friendly man, a fragile figure,
all eyes and ears – even at a very advanced age. He laughs a lot, at times complacently, sometimes
amused, even at himself. His life was full of adventurous turns. Born in Cleveland, Ohio, in 1906,
he initially studied philology, then became a curator in the architectural department of the Museum
of Modern Art in New York, did research and wrote, and set about the things he always did best –
making contacts, spotting talents, creating memorable concepts. He was one of the inventors of
labels such as "international style" and "deconstructivism". Many architects owe their careers to
him. He has, of course, himself built, the Kunsthalle in Bielefeld, Germany, for example, or the
Crystal Cathedral in Garden Grove, California. For his friend and himself, he likewise erected a
wonderful house of glass.*
It was in this house that Philip Johnson died, in January 2005.

Mr Johnson, you've ....
Don't say mister, *Herr* is fine. My German is terribly rusty, but I like your language just as much as I did 80 years ago. At that time, I used to travel to Berlin a lot. I was quite obsessed with your country.

What was it that fascinated you so much?
My curiosity was probably aroused by Nietzsche. I admired him when I was studying philosophy. Since then he's been my favourite thinker. But I'm even more enthusiastic about the Bauhaus and all the architects who decided to be done with history and set up something new. I was infected by that radicalism, the fire in the minds. The buildings of these architects opened up an unknown world for me with their white, bright, naked boxes. That world had no more dealings with the claustrophobic fug of prehistory. The burden of ornamentation and wretchedness of the nineteenth century was simply shaken off.

What about today? How do you like German architecture?
Hitler, the war, the economic collapse – it's all taken Germans' self-confidence away. None of them rank in the world league of architects. They're all too intent on doing everything by the board, so as not to be too conspicuous. You can't get great architecture with an attitude like that. You only have to look at Berlin and see what's been built there in recent years. Awful. Almost all those buildings smell of fear, Berlin is a city of fear. The last time I was there, I could scarcely bear it – so much boredom, so much lack of freedom.

But the office block you yourself built in Berlin is not exactly a model of liveliness.
Unfortunately, it isn't, you're right there. I find it frightful, too. But I let myself be pushed into that job, I'd underestimated the power of Berlin's building bureaucrats.

But still, the city's produced some things worth seeing in recent years.
Yes, there's that magnificent "blitz" by Daniel Libeskind, at any rate. And the new Chancellor's Office has something relaxed and magnificent about it. I like it, even though I know it only from pictures. Politicians here would never have allowed anything so unconventional.

Many people in Germany find the building weird, because it doesn't fit in with what they expect to see. The longing for traditional stuff is very strong. In Berlin, they're even going to rebuild the old Stadtschloss. Can you understand that?
Of course I can understand that. People want something beautiful, they want a bit of splendour in their grey city. What's more, the Schloss would be a splendid provocation to contemporary architects, some of them are quite conceited. That in itself is a good reason to look kindly on the idea of its coming back. I'm only afraid that in the end most people will be disappointed with the Schloss. It was, in fact, a wretched barracks of a place – I did see it myself. So coarse and out of proportion. Even Schinkel couldn't get on with it. I think he'd have been happier to be allowed to demolish the Schloss and build something else opposite his Altes Museum. I love Schinkel, for me he's one of the greatest. He didn't deserve to have this Baroque barn built in his name.

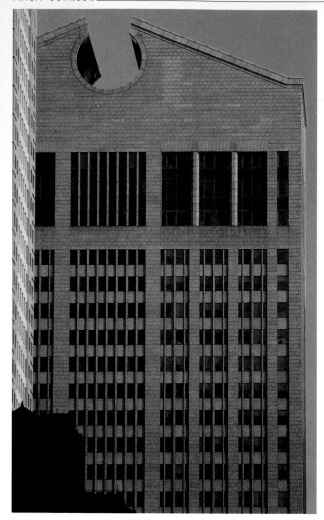

AT&T Building, New York, 1984

But your buildings have often cited history. Your AT&T building in New York is considered a torchbearer of postmodernism. Why are you now advocating that something modern be built on the Schloss site?
I'm not advocating modernism or anything else. All I find is that that Schloss was a ghastly building. I'd wish something more beautiful for Berlin.

Would it matter to you what it looked like?
Not in the least. The only important thing is, the architecture should trigger off amazement. That it should give people pleasure, cheer them up or even move them to tears. In my case, that's what happened when I visited Chartres Cathedral in Paris with my mother when I was 13. I stood there and didn't know what was happening to me. I ended up bursting into tears. If an architect can do that, or even just a bit, he's good. How he achieves it is irrelevant.

You have a reputation for always being very keen on the effect, and always changing styles. Did it never strike you that shapes and materials also mean something?
Mean? Architecture should adorn and uplift, it doesn't need meaning. It's not politics or philosophy. That was precisely the great mistake of early modernism. It thought it could mould people to a radically different life with a radically different formal idiom. It wanted to improve the world, and architecture can't do that.

What can it do, then?
It can give pleasure, it can amaze, it can ensure that people feel good. That's already quite a lot.

So architects have no social responsibility.
No, they don't. Anyone who wants to solve the many problems of mankind shouldn't be an architect but a politician or scientist. Or become a developer and build accommodation for the poor and sick – with the help of a good architect, I hope.

I'm amazed that you so casually dismiss the social ambitions of modernism. You yourself were one of the great advocates of it and first made the Bauhaus known in the USA with major architectural exhibitions in New York. Were you able to separate the aesthetic side from the ethical concern?
Obviously I could. I found Walter Gropius and his fantasies of bringing utopia to the masses suspect from the first. As far as I was concerned, modernism was mainly a style. What appealed to me was the radically new forms. I liked the revolutionary mutation, the change.

This passion for change has always been part of your life and even made you radically right-wing. First you touted the Bauhaus, a few years later you joined in Hitler's war against Poland as a reporter. How could you do U-turns so easily?
I'm afraid I didn't do any U-turns at all. I remained, in fact, very true to my love of radicalism, an aesthetic style that would permeate everything and shape everyone from scratch. There were, indeed, parallels between the Bauhaus and the Nazis. Both wanted to make history. And, of course, I wanted to be part of it. I was still very young at the time. For a time I was also very taken with Stalin. But all that is something I still regret today. These misunderstandings have pursued me all my life.

That sounds as if you'd been immunised against everything ideological.
I don't think ideology has anything to do with architecture. There's no good and no evil there. These moral questions get on my nerves.

You were always considered a heretic, and were notorious for your sharp tongue. At the same time, you compared architects to whores, and described them as just lackeys of the clients. Why were you never critical, especially after your experiences with the dictators?
But I am critical, just my buildings aren't. Architecture can't be critical at all, it can't oppose the reality it's designed for. Even Peter Eisenman doesn't believe in that sort of

thing any more. But I didn't by any means always do what clients wanted me to. They often don't know what they want. And so I was able to get them excited about things that were very unusual and spectacular. You see, I have no convictions, but do have taste.

Are you a cynic?
Why do you think that? No, I love architecture far too much for that, I'm much too euphoric for that. I've always tried to retain my curiosity. And I always gave way to that curiosity and listened to my moods. Sometimes I got involved with glass houses, then with lovely curved buildings like the Lipstick Building here in New York. I don't think anything is absolute. And that's why I find architects suspect once they find a recipe and won't let go of it any more. The ultimate truth, they call it, and dump the same things down everywhere in the world, just like that German, what's he called now? – oh, yes, Ungers. Terribly puritanical.

Don't you like the rigour?
But we're liberated of all dogmas today, relativism rules. We can do what we want. That's an exhausting freedom, and yet it's wonderful. At any rate, I can enjoy the old ideologies being dead at last. Only insecure people quickly make up new maxims they can chain themselves to. But I shouldn't be making too many remarks about my colleagues, since I'm not a good architect either.

Aren't you?
At any rate, others are much better than I am. They're much freer and more inspired in their ideas. Frank Gehry, I think he's the greatest. How important he is will really only be understood in fifty years' time. I've always had time for people like him, people I knew had more talent than I did. I supported Gehry and Eisenman, the young ones, even though they, too, are already over 70 now.

Many people accused Gehry of doing art, not architecture.
Those critics have no idea. Architecture is art, nothing else. Of course it has to fulfil many functions. But instead of form following function, it's the other way round. I'm always interested primarily in what people feel in my buildings, what they notice, what mood it creates in them. That's what I have to think about, not escape routes, cable ducts and porches. Those are things my partner thinks about, he's the practical one. If I had to do that myself, it would ruin all my pleasure in architecture.

Is it that pleasure that drives you to go on doing new buildings? You could actually stop and look back proudly on your rich life's work – why don't you?
To be honest, I get in a pretty bad state if I don't have a project I can wrap my mind round. It's like being buried alive. I once tried it out for a bit, it didn't work.

Is there something you look for in work?
No, there's no search involved. It's change I want. When I'm designing a building, it gives me an opportunity to change myself, try out something new. I think that's the

quintessence of life. And if I can't sense that, I needn't bother to get up any more. So I still get myself driven to the office, discuss things with my people, work up some new ideas, even though it's getting more and more difficult. It's terrible to be trapped in such an old body.

Much as you like change, you've still stuck to some things. You still live in the glass house you built more than 50 years ago in Connecticut – it was your exam piece. Why haven't you ever moved?
I've never thought about it. Perhaps because this building keeps surprising me, it keeps giving me pleasure every day. Why should I look for another one?

Glass House, New Canaan, Connecticut, 1949

REM KOOLHAAS

BUT NEUTRALITY DOESN'T INTEREST ME, WHAT INTERESTS ME IS COMPLEXITY

Born in Rotterdam in 1944, Rem Koolhaas is one of the few architects who is known worldwide not so much for his designs as for his books. He had already made himself somewhat of a reputation with his Manhattan theory – Delirious New York of 1978 – but the breakthrough came with the mighty tome S, M, L, XL of 1995. Important architectural commissions, for example, the Kunsthal in Rotterdam, came the way of his architectural practice OMA even earlier. But his global career as an architect did not really begin until the late 1990s. The office workforce mushroomed from 12 to 250 – and Koolhaas, lean and gangling, now looks even more harassed than ever. For years now, he has spent more time in aeroplanes and hotels than at home in London or in his office in Rotterdam. His jobs are in New York, or Singapore or Dubai. Best-known of all are his Dutch embassy in Berlin, his library for Seattle and the Casa da Música in Oporto. His biggest job came from China, where he is building an audacious skyscraper. But writing and researching remain important for him. Through his second firm, AMO, he advises museums, fashion companies, even the EU. Koolhaas has gone on expanding the architect's brief – he wants to be everything at once – screenplay writer, teacher, politician and, you've guessed, constructor of buildings.

Mr Koolhaas, avant-garde buildings have never before been as popular as they are today. Is this the beginning of a golden age for architects?
I think that what we're experiencing is the global triumph of eccentricity. Lots of extravagant buildings are being built, buildings that have no meaning, no functionality. It's rather about spectacular shapes and, of course, the architects' egos.

Does this surprise you?
It does amaze me. The world of architecture has radically changed in only 15 years.

Why is that?
That's because the media and architecture are more than ever before totally dependent on one another.

Is it the media's fault?
Who was it that invented the term "star architects"? It was the media with their grotesque greed for sensations and exciting images. The expectations of architects changed enormously because of it. They're not expected to design well-thought-out, complex buildings any more, symbols are what's wanted, icons that are marketed through the media.

Is that something new? Even the Bauhaus architects used the media to promote their buildings. The Eiffel Tower and the Sydney Opera House were already icons in their time.
But these days everything is now decided by the last ideology we still have, the ideology of the market. Fifteen years ago it was taken for granted that architects worked for public clients, i.e., their eye was on the public benefit. That social dimension of architecture has meantime almost disappeared, as the state has retreated. The most important jobs come from private clients, and they see architecture only as a form of advertising, a source of profit, everything else is irrelevant.

But all the new museums and concert halls are financed by public clients.
In the end it amounts to the same thing, because lots of cities also suffer from the attention-grabbing syndrome and only follow commercial logic. In fact, they don't invest in culture but in effect and marketing.

Still, many clients today have an astonishing appetite for risk. They let themselves in for architectural experiments that even ten years ago were inconceivable.
OK, architects have more freedom than ever, there are more opportunities today. But paradoxically, each of these opportunities conceals many more limitations than before. Think of the fantastic new estates that J. J. P. Oud managed to build. He designed not just a few façades but also laid down how many schools, churches and shops were also needed in one area.

And you hunger for this omnipotence?
Not at all, not even in moments of weakness. Who still believes in architects as the inspired creators of new worlds? I can't see any utopian model that would still be work-

able, nothing on which an architect can orientate himself by. What then remains for the architect but for him to design pretty ornaments and that's it?

Tell us.
I have no answer. All I can say is that I am interested in content, in structures, in that which architecture is really made up of.

What does architecture amount to?
The same questions have been asked ever since the Enlightenment. How do we want to live? What opportunities does modernism offer us with its liberties and technical progress? Ultimately, what makes us happy?

Are your buildings a promise of happiness?
Well, that's a question you will have to answer. After all, you're the critic.

I'd like to hear it from you.
I'd rather keep quiet. No architect can presume to be able to prescribe or even define happiness. Though, of course, I can't get along without ideals and a certain degree of optimism. Well OK, perhaps OMA architecture can indeed make many people happy, not by decreeing they be happy but by overcoming constraints. It doesn't force you to waste time and energy, in fact, it sets something free and opens up spaces.

That sounds rather nebulous.
No, not at all, it's very specific. Think of Dubai, for example, where fantastic puberty buildings are going up at present. We're planning something serious and adult there, a district that will be as urban as possible. In Dubai, everyone goes by car, even from one building to the next. Where we're building, you can walk, there'll be a metro, we're mixing homes and offices – everything to break down the autism of the architecture.

If you're planning a whole new quarter, do you have an ideal image at the back of your mind?
If I dream, it's of places that should be as accessible and public as possible. But I tend to resist ideal images, they just wouldn't work in Dubai at all. This job is actually very abstract, because we don't know how society there is going to develop, who's going to live and work there, or what needs the area has to satisfy.

Does that mean you have to plan things as open-ended and indeterminate as possible?
You could say that.

So really you ought to be planning neutral boxes.
But neutrality doesn't interest me, what interests me is complexity. I like buildings that are not authoritarian, but that leave as many options open as possible. Whether anyone makes use of these options remains open, of course. As an architect, I can only make them available, that's all.

And what part do externals play – the design? You haven't said anything about that.
There's a patent artistic component in all our projects. But I find there's not much you can usefully say about it.

Why not?
Because it's mainly a matter of feelings. We're very interested in how people react to our buildings, what resonance they have for them. But if I were to explain now in an interview what you should or could feel in the buildings, it would be absurd. Architecture would then just be nothing more than a theme park with programmed feelings and pre-set moods.

I only ask because you often sound as if building were mainly a matter of structure, something very rational.
No, good architecture is always both – very rational and very irrational.

The Bordeaux Villa, 1998

Many of your buildings look positively surreal.
There is that dimension, it's true. I feel Surrealism influences me, though mostly sub-consciously. And that's where it can certainly remain, in the subconscious. Talking about it gets us nowhere.

Would you call your building for Chinese Central Television in Beijing surrealist?
It does have something oddly disconcerting about it. It only struck me when the build-ing was up and the tilting towers were joined together. It's the only building I know which is both foreground and background. It's entirely itself, but it remains in contact. It goes with the urban context. I also like its monumental fragility, which sometimes looks beautiful, sometimes odd.

To me, it looks most of all like one of those icons you like so much.
Of course, any building of that size always has a symbolic side, that can't be avoided. But it's not one of those two-dimensional sticker images, it has an enormous number of different angles to it, it always looks different, depending on where you're looking from.

That almost sounds as if you were formulating a kind of political broadcasting specifica-tion – seeing the world from many angles, not just the view prescribed by state TV.
Nice that you see it that way.

Do you see it like that, too?
Ah now, I don't want to pin the building down to any kind of message.

You avoid anything definite.
That's it. I have a tendency towards claustrophobia.

Literally or metaphorically?
Both, I think.

But even if you want to leave the defining contexts as open-ended as possible – you'd scarcely deny that a political building like this also makes a political statement, would you?
(pause) It is probably inevitably political.

And does that mean that your architecture is taken over politically? Or expressed more directly – are you making a pact with a dictatorship?
Just a moment. *(Jumps up, hurries out of the room, and disappears for two or three minutes, then returns with a book).* Here, you need to read that. *What Does China Think?*, by Mark Leonard, a friend of mine.

You mean, I'll find an answer to my question in it.
You'll understand why it's wrong to condemn China simply as a dictatorship. The coun-try has come an enormously long way in recent years and made great progress. Within a very short time, a wholly underdeveloped economic system as been reformed, and along with that a lot of rights have developed, for example, the right to own property.

And what about human rights, the right to freedom of opinion, for example?
Of course, there's still a lot to do, the question for me is only how to achieve it. And that's where I think it's rather fatuous for the West to be always just criticising. The West is critical, forever critical. Constant criticism like that just leads up a blind alley.

Why's that?
Because the West can't act as if it still possessed global hegemony. At the moment we're experiencing a drastic shift, powers are suddenly shifting towards China, South-East Asia, the Arab countries. Pure non-democracies are gaining influence.

That's the very reason for holding up the values of democracy.
But you don't get anywhere with moral arrogance. That only leads to polarisation, and that's unproductive. We have to admit that the rights of the individual that are so sacred to us have no tradition in countries such as China. And that there are therefore also cultural differences as far as having a say and protesting are concerned. There are, in fact, a lot of Chinese who protest about the demolition of old houses or against the construction of dams. Only it's often differently from the way we do things here. Open conflict is avoided.

Or all the protesters are locked up in prison. Was it at all a moral issue for you whether you should accept the CCTV job?
Of course it was a moral issue. What do you think? I'm not a cynic.

And why did you decide to accept the job in the end?
I've just tried to explain that. If there is a possibility of collaboration, one should accept it. Because any collaboration means getting involved with other people, with their rules and ways of thinking. Only that way, I think, can things be changed.

So what exactly has changed as a result of the CCTV project?
They're slow, invisible changes, of course. And I'd find it completely crazy to expect that China would become like us from one day to the next. It took democracy several hundred years to develop in Europe. Nevertheless, it seems to me that it is especially the progressive forces that show up in our building. For example, it's being discussed just now at CCTV whether state television should be divided up into a traditional part and a modern part based mostly on the pattern of the BBC. And the modern, enlightened TV people would then move into our building. In all modesty, for me the building seems to mark a change.

Would you build for other dictatorships as well, for North Korea, for example?
If the New York Philharmonic perform in North Korea, that's also taken as a sign of rapprochement and international understanding. Why do architects have to justify themselves?

The CCTV building during construction, 2008

Perhaps because architects, given our experience of the twentieth century, are suspected of glorifying power.
But we don't glorify, we allow ourselves the freedom to develop our own unusual ideas. And only if a client allows us this freedom do we accept the job. That's why the question doesn't even arise as to whether we would build in North Korea. Because there is no offer of collaboration on the table, the country is not open and doesn't seek contact. And that distinguishes it from China.

And your conscience is not touched by the fact that, in China, slave-like migrant workers are employed for many of the large-scale products projects, including the CCTV building?
There are a lot of things that I don't like in China. But I think we have to be pragmatic. It is, of course, easy to imagine the present development in China going wrong. And that's what a lot of people in the West think, they don't believe in a positive development. It seems to me more intelligent to imagine a positive development.

Time and again, you've taken up negative subjects and turned them into positive subjects. You've written a weighty volume about shopping, you've become engrossed in the faceless outskirts of cities, and you've investigated urban chaos in Nigeria. What makes you do that?
There's no rule that says architecture should build only beautiful buildings. I'm simply interested in what one might call reality, the airports, the industrial areas, the suburbs. I should just like to get as neutral a picture as possible of how things stand in our world. I want to describe and analyse, without immediately passing judgement.

Could one say you have remained true to your journalistic beginnings?
I don't think just to them.

What else?
I worked not only as a journalist, I also wrote screenplays. And sometimes it seems to me that working on a building is like writing a screenplay. It's all a matter of tension, atmosphere, rhythm, the right sequence of spatial impressions.

If you were to film your own life, where would you begin?
Perhaps completely conventionally, with my childhood.

Why?
Because that was a very eventful time for me. I grew up in a city that wasn't there any more, in Rotterdam, which had been completely devastated by the Germans. For children, of course, a great place for discoveries. Then when I was eight, we moved to Indonesia, where again everything was on the move, as the country had just become independent. I also learnt Indonesian, was a Scout there and all that. I assume I have that period to thank for my Asiatic vein.

Your Asiatic vein?
Well, when we came back to Rotterdam, everything there was orderly, straight and clean, as terribly boring as many cities look today, which are actually not cities but suburbs. I noticed at the time how much I'd liked it in Indonesia, how provisional and unfinished everything was there. How lively chaos is, for example, the markets, all the trading and haggling is done beneath an open sky. Anyone who's ever experienced that will find our sterile shopping zones unappealing.

You mean, you felt more of a foreigner in your native city than in Indonesia?
I don't know. I simply liked being able to look at the world from outside, as someone to whom not everything appeared a matter of course. And in a certain sense that is still part of our method here in the office, as far as possible beginning every job from scratch and forgetting everything you think you know. That's how we did it in Seattle, when it depended on getting a new idea of what a library can be today. Or in Oporto, where we thought long and hard about other functions and shapes for a concert hall.

That almost sounds as if you didn't even build these buildings.
We did build them. But building always means to me research, sort of thinking around and questioning.

Building as criticism?
I don't think that architecture can be critical or subversive. There are architects that see that otherwise, Peter Eisenman, for example. He calls it subversive when his walls are slightly slanting. Subversion is simply a new form of style, nothing more.

Would you define yourself as a conventional architect?

(laughs) No, not really. Perhaps one can say that I see building as a pragmatic form of criticism, as a mutual learning process, although that's not always entirely easy to keep up. It's a paradoxical situation: you want to keep a critical distance and at the same time get immersed in a project. Not infrequently, we had to get involved in things where we didn't exactly know at all whether anything sensible would come out of it. Whether our questions could be made productive and be turned into a design. For a time, for example, I was convinced that cities couldn't be sensibly planned. We'd examined Lagos, a huge city, which organises itself completely and gets by very well without any planners and architects, which seemed to me very symptomatic for urban planning as a whole. Yet time and again we were asked to work on cities, develop plans, and we got involved in these projects without really being able to believe in them.

Out of pleasure in failure?

No, what mattered to us was questioning ourselves and our external perspectives, because only when you get involved in a project can you judge what room for manoeuvre there is. And incidentally, that's how we fared in Lagos. Meantime there are many indications that it's city planners who have created the conditions for self-organising urban development. It really needs both for a vital city, planned and un-planned elements. Together they produce the necessary tension.

Does that apply to your own work as well, to the tension between theory and practice?

At any rate, we try to cultivate this tension systematically. For a time, that was very difficult, because we wanted to bring all our critical deliberations into the design with every project. A few years ago, we opened a second firm alongside OMA called AMO, our research office, a kind of thinking factory.

Does that mean you've divided yourself into Jekyll & Hyde? Jekyll builds, Hyde thinks?

(laughs) Jekyll doesn't know anything about Hyde, nor Hyde anything about Jekyll, so that's the difference between us. A lot of what goes on at AMO also goes into the designs. But it allows us an incredible freedom, to be able to think about things system-atically, without immediately having to build. There's a great need for architectural thought over and beyond specific projects.

You are an adviser to Prada as well as to the European Union. Are you the McKinsey of the architectural industry?

With normal advisers, it's only a matter of increasing profits. We are not interested in that, we don't even understand anything about that. Basically, what it's about, as far as we're concerned, is propaganda for non-material values. It's rather like in art, which likewise has its financial side and yet actually lives from its content and aesthetics. We are interested in that content and the aesthetics.

The Seattle Public Library, 2004

What sort of content is involved when you advise Prada? Anything more than fashion and turnover?
Of course about those as well, but not just those. For example, it's about public space, i.e., the question as to whether fashion shops can be more than fashion shops. For example, whether there could be a lecture hall or a gallery or any other kind of cultural meeting point.

To me, it seems more like a sophisticated marketing strategy if a boutique puts itself across as a public space or cultural centre.
That may seem to be the case at first glance, but many themes that we smuggle in during our commissions then develop a life of their own. And if in partnership with

Prada we manage to draw attention to public space, so that it seems something important, indeed precious, why should there be anything bad about that?

You're a romantic.
How so?

In the end, you do believe you can change the world with your architecture.
(laughs) Okay, in that sense I'm a romantic. But the Romantic spirit, the artist hero, has
long since abdicated.

But anyone who considers the EU capable of listening must indeed be a hero.
I'm now interested in ideas. And I find that most Europeans, and even the EU itself,
know too little about their own ideas, or one might say their own ideals. I like the fact
that the Europeans are not trying to create a Super State. They rather want to maintain
their differences as much as possible, declare their differences as a virtue. But most
Europeans don't even want to know how amazing, how delightfully complex that is.
That's why we're thinking about looking for new kinds of narratives for these ideas.
That's all the more important as the EU has hitherto always been perceived as a community of economic interests. Which means to say, when the market economy comes
to an end, then the alliance is in grave danger, unless we finally understand its actual
values. Currently, the semi-dictatorships of the world are economically very successful,
a model that, of course, seems very attractive even to many people here in the West.

Is the market economy then really at its end?
It is obvious that the market is failing in many areas. The economy is growing and
growing, and yet we're no longer able to afford many of the things that were easily
affordable just a few decades ago. I don't in the least mean by that just architecture,
which is coming under increasing cost pressures and has to be produced more and
more cheaply. Just look at our health system or the schools and universities or public
swimming pools – in many areas, we're unable to keep up the standards of the past
despite the fact that more and more money is being earned.

And new narratives should change something about that?
No, we can only try to draw attention to deficits of that sort and also to our unrecog-
nised strengths. Perhaps it begins with turning our own contradictions to good advantage. Look, China has it easy there, it is neither clearly communist nor clearly capitalist.
The country is a hybrid, and that's one reason why it's so successful. It is more difficult
for Europe, as it sees in itself mainly the bureaucratic monster. The complexity of
this alliance is really astonishing, even the systematics that it works with, over and
beyond the normal political show. In a certain sense, the bureaucracy itself could be
considered an immense success that does much for the peaceful coexistence of states
in this world.

How so?

Via the standards and regulations that it sets up. There's a book of regulations that, when printed, makes a book some 23 feet thick. These rules are also taken over by countries outside the EU, and not only when these countries want to trade with EU countries, but also if they negotiate among themselves, for example, when Alaska trades with Morocco. The European system creates reliability, it defines forms of collaboration, not through armies but through regulations. I find that a surprising discovery.

Is that what you particularly like in your profession – surprise?

The day doesn't pass when I am not surprised, even at myself.

And is it never too much for you?

Sometimes it is.

And then?

Then I disappear from sight.

Where?

I swim every day, often for an hour or two. Regardless of where I am, I always look for a swimming pool.

Swimming pools as a refuge?

No, the last resort of a classless utopia. You simply jump in, everyone's naked and not having the usual support, you just go along with it. If I want to understand a country, I only have to go to a swimming pool there.

DANIEL LIBESKIND

THIS BUILDING TELLS A STORY

How do you build history? Or construct meaning? And the big issue: how can you talk of Auschwitz with architecture, and speak the unspeakable? Those were the questions that faced Libeskind when he was drawing up plans for the Jewish Museum in Berlin in 1988. Since then, memory and sorrow, emptiness and brokenness have become themes of many of his buildings. Not least because he himself, born in 1946, has personally experienced many of the twentieth century's snubs. Libeskind was born in Łódź, but emigrated with his parents initially to Israel, then to the USA, where he studied music and for quite a while lived from his talent as a pianist. But then he opted for architecture and especially architectural theory. Understanding the philosophical background long seemed to him more important than doing the building, but in the end many major commissions still came his way, for example, a war museum in Manchester and an art museum in Denver. Finally he was given the huge task of planning Ground Zero in New York (even if in the end not much remains of his master plan). People normally look askance at philosophically minded, intellectual architects, but Libeskind is always so good-humoured, always beaming, always laughing and youthfully engaging that he has been able to win over numerous clients.

Mr Libeskind, one of your astonishing buildings is the Jewish Museum in Berlin. That was visited by more than 350,000 people before it even opened. Many people still find the architecture so eloquent they think there's no need for an exhibition.
The empty building was an exhibition in itself, you're right. And I was, of course, glad that many people identified with the building in an intellectual and emotional way. But without all the many exhibits of the Jewish Museum, in the long term the emptiness would have predominated, so that the building would have been much too focused on the loss, on the extinction of Jewish culture. After all, it's not a Holocaust museum.

Many of the exhibition organisers do complain about the zigzag building, though. Why didn't you take their needs into account more?
The building isn't a conventional box, of course, but it's simply not true that curators have particular problems there.

You wouldn't deny that your building is making a distinctly didactic point.
It's not didactic, it's very open. Everyone is invited to form his own image of the building and what it represents. There are many interpretations. Architecture's like a text that's constantly being reinterpreted, sometimes perceptively, sometimes wide of the mark, sometimes intelligently. In every case, people feel that this building tells a story, but not a one-dimensional one ending in a full stop.

Isn't there the danger that your eloquent, very emotional architecture will turn every visit to the Jewish Museum into a kind of adventure tour, a trip to the Holocaust theme park? Why do you dramatise something that is dramatic anyway?
Those really are cynical accusations. Anyone who feels he has a problem with the commercialisation of the Holocaust overlooks the fact that very many people are interested in the Shoah. They want to know what happened in those years. And they don't see the past as something that's done with, but ask what the effects on our present-day life have been. Of course, many critics would like to dismiss the building as kitsch, as a sham, something artificial. But I don't know of any visitors who found my architecture as lacking in credibility. Quite the reverse, most are surprised by the earnestness, and the complexity of the building, too. That's why it's so popular.

Do you mean your building is sober and reticent?
No, not that. But I never wanted to simulate anything. Nothing is further from my mind than a Jewish theme park. But at the same I did think it important to leave room for emotions as well. Many people stand in the Holocaust Tower of the Museum and feel grief and consternation, while others see it as a spiritual space and talk of hope. Everyone can probe their own feelings there and reflect on what they've seen, heard and read in the Museum.

Jewish Museum, view towards underground roads, Berlin, 1999

But is architecture done with relish, maybe even sensuous, appropriate for the purpose?
People should also enjoy the museum and feel comfortable in it, otherwise it would be just a memorial descended on once a year for an official memorial service.

A museum as a place people like going to?
Yes, absolutely. That's not how I'd put it for a memorial, but for a museum, yes. I was not aiming to design claustrophobic or fatalistic spaces. There is light, too, and an outlook on the future and the humane side. So the building is not fixated on the Holocaust. There's a broad spectrum of moods. The incredible high points of German-Jewish culture and history in Berlin also come across.

That sounds as if you wanted a harmonious balance.
Of course I didn't design a museum to satisfy the soul, or one that claims that all wounds are healed by time. The Holocaust was not a short-term disruption of the small screen but a break that changed everything, everything in Germany and everything for Jews. Even though Jewish history goes on, of course, and people look for a brighter future, a shadow will remain for all the brightness. I think that can also be sensed by every visitor to my museum.

But what exactly do people sense there? And what makes them sense it?
It's the same with the power of architecture as with the power of words – it's difficult to say how it works. I only know that it works very directly, you don't have to be able to read or be educated. The building influences visitors through its rooms and materials, it points to particular things and determines the way in which they see the exhibition. It's not a black box, but asserts its own reality. And thereby lends the past a solid presence. History is not virtual, but something that has been thought out. That's the message of my architecture.

Many people describe the effectiveness of your building as magical or mystical. Do you mystify the Holocaust?
Definitely not. I simply try to translate a dimension of our history into architecture that one would probably have to describe as paradoxical and incomprehensible – that one cannot rejoice at the achievements of Moses Mendelssohn without remembering at the same time what happened to his family. It's like in the music of Schoenberg, where you come across a tonality in a melodic whole that cuts straight through your experiences. Suddenly you feel entranced, transported and bemused. To that extent, my architecture is not an intellectual superstructure either, but provokes feelings of distraction and lends the museum depth. It's not just about fun and obvious things – though it's those as well, but the invisible also becomes visible here just as much.

So, museums as churches or something?
The museum is a secular building. Not even history arises from some mythical, primeval causes. But then again, belief and religion are part of history and, as such, also part of my architectural design.

But why does architecture have to play such an important role in the first place? Why don't you exercise greater restraint?
Not even a rectangular box is a neutral building. Architecture of that kind wouldn't please me, there would be something depressing about it for me because it was so lifeless and bereft of all ideas. How can a building that is wholly reduced in its external appearance tell you something about the complexity of our history and the present day? The richness of reality, and maybe its contradictions, are smoothed out there. I can't be doing with attempts at rationalisation such as Peter Zumthor, for example, envisaged for the Nazi Topography of Terror museum. For me, architecture always has to be an expression of a quest, something to express research and enquiry. After all, we shall never know conclusively what was real in the past. We only think we know.

Your museum is so expressive and multifaceted that it was proposed turning it into a Holocaust memorial. Could you have imagined that?
The museum does indeed absolutely possess elements of a memorial, the Holocaust Tower, for example, or the voids. And probably no Jewish museum at this location would pass muster without memorial rooms of that kind. In the end, it's not just a matter of simply exhibiting a few beautiful, valuable exhibits here.

Is the museum therefore a place of mourning?
I've never thought much about that. Many people might see it as such. For me, the museum is principally an emblem of hope. It's proof that future generations will also conserve our history and take it seriously. So the museum doesn't deal just with our past, otherwise it would indeed be only an ossified memorial, a place of retrospect. No, this museum is more like a living organism, nothing is sealed off, nothing is final. It's also about what is to come.

Is reconciliation your objective?
That's a word that means nothing to me. My objective was to build a kind of disruptive element into my architecture of the exhibition. People should enjoy themselves in the Jewish Museum, they should feel good and be impressed. But I wanted to prevent them escaping into nostalgia, into the good old days that have nothing more to do with the present.

But can you inspire memory with your architecture? The powerful symbolic idiom of your building above all tends to make personal access difficult.
You mean the shattered Star of David? The zigzag thunderbolt? But they are all symbols that don't exist. Many people just thought them up because they can't bear the openness and lack of symbolic signs in my architecture. But the building resists such premature attributions and one-dimensional interpretations. This museum is, after all, not

ewish Museum, exterior view, Berlin, 1999

about deNazification either, or crudely stated doctrines. Nor is it about a compulsory educational course, knowledge that has to be drummed into people. The aim is to open up an opportunity to delve deeper into history. There are no pre-formulated metaphors, but there are many things that can be appropriated and empathised with. Of course, memory can't be switched on and off like a TV, but perhaps the architecture is nevertheless successful in acting as a catalyst, reinforcing memory and steering it in many directions at once. That would be my wish, anyway – that people leave this museum with an experience that means something to them. That they don't remain uninvolved.

Jewish Museum, interior of Holocaust void, Berlin, 1999

GREG LYNN

ALL ARCHITECTURE IS AN EXPRESSION OF HOMESICKNESS

Los Angeles has its own Serenissima, a district called Venice. It's peaceful here, though a bit over-grown. Greg Lynn's little house is hidden behind a tall, rampant hedge, and behind the house is a kind of two-storey garage. Downstairs, children's toys and rocking chairs; above, a tiny office stuffed full with computers and models, with the architect in the middle. A gangling, near six-footer, at ease and summery, with a wild mop of hair and sophisticated, lightweight glasses – one could take him for one of those Californian prodigies of the virtual world for whom the meaning of life lies solely in the expanses of the digital network. However, the success this architect, born 1964, has had is very real. He has long been a leading figure of the younger generation in the search for new, unseen forms and spaces. And the establishment – theory heavyweights such as Peter Eisenman and Rem Koolhaas – afford him respect and have accepted him as on par with them. He has already managed to build a number of highly regarded buildings, a church in New York, for example. But he is still content with the backyard garage, dance music pounding out of large loudspeakers, and the casual life. On the veranda there are two rusty armchairs with steel webbing. We sit down.

How come you live in a building that looks quite normal and even a bit boring? You're considered a radical innovator!
You overlook the fact that this building is actually a paradise. Just like this whole district of Los Angeles, which is called Venice and was built as a pleasure park and paradise. They dug out canals everywhere at the time, and artificial nature was the result. The buildings were built ready-made in a factory, delivered by a chain store by rail and erected on the spot. This cute little bungalow I live in is, therefore, in reality a radical innovation of the twenties. I'd love to claim that radicalism for myself. Even if in fifty years' time it looked nostalgic and cute like this house. We can't escape the necessity of the new.

Why not? We could be satisfied with the tried and tested.
Of course, all architecture is an expression of homesickness and therefore nostalgia as well. But I find it unacceptable even to recycle this nostalgia. No, the good old days were not as good as people think. The future won't be so grand either. But we have no other choice than to go on trying to improve the world by doing new things.

What would be an improvement?
People want buildings that reflect the ideas of our time. But architecture always acts as if it were timeless. Or it takes cover and tries to be as invisible as possible.

Is fashionable architecture what you want?
I've nothing against fashion. I think architecture should be treated much more like music or painting. Only then will it regain its relevance and become important for our identity.

That sounds as if architecture were like new sunglasses you put on when you don't like the old ones any more.
It's difficult to compete with the importance of the right sunglasses! But why not? You see, I want architecture to be socially as relevant as, for example, the Beatles. In their day, they gave voice to a whole attitude to life. Even today, you keep hearing them. Even so, no one would think of just copying the Beatles sound. Only in architecture do people still think that what's already been achieved can be continued for ever. That's where most architects underestimate the fact that they're not constructing neutral shells with their buildings but helping to determine the atmosphere. So a building makes a subtle mark on people that's difficult to describe. But the more we take these subtleties into account, the more important architecture becomes again in ordinary life. It becomes more authentic.

Do you feel untouched by history?
No, not at all. I don't think it's about creating a vacuum in which everything would have to be invented from scratch. I think about Alberti, for example – his stipulation that a good building is one nothing can be added to, but also nothing removed. How do you design something like that? That's the kind of theoretical interest that gets me investigating things.

At the Venice Biennale a few years ago you constructed a kind of research laboratory. What were you looking for there?
You mean my Embryological House, a research project, supported by state grants and art museums. What I have in mind is buildings that tally with a contemporary understanding of body. But I don't want to build this just for a few venturesome patrons. My objective is mass production, but without the usual monotony of pre-fabricated buildings. Industrial CNC machines allow us an incredible degree of individualisation. An infinite number of variations is quite conceivable.

These are very adaptable forms, soft and organic. Are you aiming for a natural, earthbound architecture?
Like in an ecosystem, the individual parts of my buildings should be in a relationship of interdependence – so that changing one part leads to a change in all the other parts. In a way, there are parallels there between building and cooking, since both are processes in which everything combines with everything else, changes, and in the end becomes a shared whole.

Are you looking for harmony, a new unity of the spheres?
That's what separates my generation from people such as Peter Eisenman or Rem Koolhaas. We're not afraid of holistic concepts. My buildings should be as harmonious as classical architecture was. But I don't want their rigorous order, but more of a movable, interactive structure.

Why harmonious?
Because order becomes visible in harmony, as does beauty. And that's what architecture is about – order and beauty.

Down with deconstructivism?
Two years ago, Frank Gehry dropped in once because he'd heard that we were working on things like that. Then he saw my models and said in surprise: "No, we're not doing the same – your things look harmonious." Our forms are similar, but our interests are different. Which is perhaps a matter of generations.

A conflict of generations?
I'm no longer interested in the quest for new ways of disrupting order. Nor can I be doing with postmodernism or with architecture that strives solely for fragmentation. What I'm looking for instead is new methods of organisation, and I'm carried along by the utopianism of the sixties. Architecture has to join the mainstream again and adopt the reality of other arts.

Like in Art Nouveau?
Modern architecture began with the total design of that time. Natural forms became more important than the classical stylistic conventions. At the same time, industrial manufacturing processes came to the fore – another similarity with my work. Though I'm not involved with the style or the forms of that time.

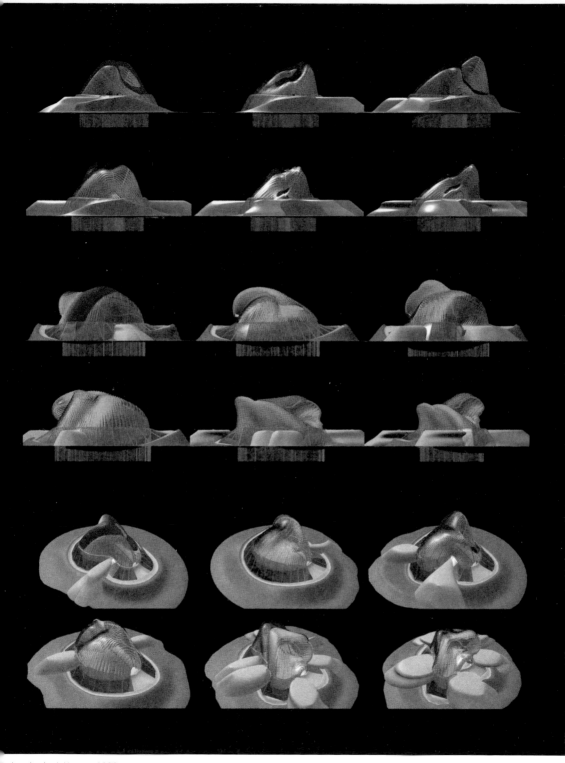

Embryological House, 1998

Many early heroes of modernism wanted to turn society upside down. Do you?
I don't think the social issue is where it starts, it's more a part of the design process.
That's where you get to see how social problems can be countered with architectural
solutions.

Some critics say beautiful shapes are all that matter to you.
There's this remarkable prejudice that an architect who thinks form is important is not
bothered with social concerns, as if there could only be one or the other. It would be
more honest of the critics to openly stick by their rejection of forms instead of asserting
that consciously formal architecture is not functional or isn't going down a socially
relevant road.

What does a design begin with for you?
The question for me is always, how do I move about in a building and what do I notice
when I move about in it? One should notice a change of rhythm like in music, linking
all the elements. I think first of all about the interior life of the building, after that I
move on to how the interior relates to the setting.

Is that withdrawing into the private sphere?
Maybe. But perhaps it's also a reaction to my experiences with Peter Eisenman. I
worked for him for ages. There, the first thing was always the distribution of mass,
a rough articulation of the exterior. The interiors were always just a by-product.

**The first building you actually built is a church in New York. It looks quite different from the
computer drawings. How do you explain that?**
On the computer I just try out new design techniques. On the other hand, many people
try to build so that the buildings look the way they do on the computer – fluid, soft and
smooth. I tend to prefer sliced off and perforated effects, complexity. Also, in the design
the church looked like a huge bubble and so got changed.

**Your office is stuffed full of computers. It looks as if you could just as well have been an
inventor of video games.**
Even before I was born, my parents decided I was to be an architect. My mother read
somewhere that Frank Lloyd Wright had been trained to be an architect from earliest
childhood, and when I was a child I went on all kinds of courses. Then when I got
to college, I was so bored by most of the structural seminars that I did my degree in
philosophy.

So how come architecture after all?
Crazily enough, the thing that interested me most in philosophy was the history of
geometry, so taking a step back wasn't difficult. But even now I see myself as shuttling
between the two. Time, space and motion are still philosophical questions for me.

Crossing frontiers with the computer?
From the eighteenth century on, the division of labour was quite clear. The architect invents the forms, while the engineer can analyse and calculate them. Computers have abolished this distinction, reinforcing our intuitions. Wholly new forms are being turned out.

What kind?
I want buildings that have grown. Because you know at once whether an object has been shaped by time or not.

A growing house.
On the computer, the building goes through a process that resembles a growth process. Naturally that's limited to the design phase, when we get all possible variables to interact at once. Out of that you get a form that is very complex and organic in appearance. It's all very precisely tailored to the user's wishes.

But the question of how our cities look in future and could develop plays no particular part in that.
I haven't had much time to think of such questions. Of course, the subject of the urban scene is important, but I always think first of buildings and only then of the urban structure. It's a long time since I thought about specific models, pure research has been my interest.

OSCAR NIEMEYER

MUCH MORE IMPORTANT THAN ARCHITECTURE TO ME ARE LIFE, FRIENDS AND FAMILY

Though a centenarian, he still goes to his studio every day, high above the glittering waves of Copacabana. Faxes and letters, enquiries and contracts pile up his desk every day. Oscar Niemeyer is a public person, a much revered, violently hated one – the last surviving co-founder of modernism. Why don't we talk about literature, he says, about the universe, about women? And then nonetheless he talks about his century, about the years of radical forms and the yearning for change. Born in Rio in 1907, the son of a German-born immigrant, he studied architecture, and worked together with Le Corbusier on the design for the new Ministry of Education, the first public monument of modernism in Latin America. Where people in Europe trusted in reason, Niemeyer went for feeling. Earlier than anyone else, back in 1940, in fact, he turned against monotone, functionalist buildings. He became a popular hero when he put a face on the sweeping, soaring concrete fabric of the new capital, Brasilia. Unfortunately, he was forced into emigration in France shortly after, because even then he was a member of the Communist Party and was afraid of the new rulers of Brazil. He built a party headquarters for the Communist Party in Paris, and the monumental sculptural building for Mondadori in Milan. But Rio was always his home, and he soon returned. On his hundredth birthday, he was celebrated there like a particularly popular tribune.

You've achieved everything in your life an architect can achieve. But you still go on building new buildings. Why?

You know, getting so old is rather shitty. But what else is there left to me now I'm so old? So I go on, since I haven't learnt anything else. Though you're mistaken if you think that only architecture is important to me. I still plan this project or that project, letters and faxes arrive every day, and people ask me for new designs. But much more important than architecture to me are life, friends and family.

What was it that made it you become an architect?

I've always liked drawing and done it a lot. It seems to have been inbred in me. As a child, I often did drawings in the air. When I did, my mother asked me what it was I was doing. Drawing, I said. At school, I got top marks in art, I can still remember that clearly. And my mother kept all my drawings, I'm very pleased about that. A nice memory.

So why didn't you become an artist rather than an architect?

Perhaps I still am that child drawing. *(laughs)* I sit here at my desk, all alone with my pencil and a sheet of paper and draw whatever comes to mind. My colleagues do the rest, they're terrifically hardworking.

Do you find there's no difference between architecture and art?

Oh yes, certainly there is. Architecture is not a detached, free art. Everything in it is connected to everything else, and that attracted me very much. That's why I tell students who visit me, it's not your degree that matters, you need to know the world and your country. Architecture is nothing if it doesn't have anything to do with this country, with beauty and all the problems.

Did you want to change the world with your architecture, then?

My parents had a country estate, so I grew up very protected, we didn't even go to the fair, because we had one at home with the neighbours. So when I was older and got to know the world, I was terrified, because it seemed false and degenerate to me. You see, I had a clear notion deep inside me what a peaceful, just world ought to be like. Even before I enrolled as an architectural student, I became a member of the Communist Party.

Shortly after graduating, you met Le Corbusier in Rio. What did you learn from him?

He'd come to Rio by Zeppelin to design the Ministry of Education, and I was able to help him somewhat with the drawings. It was a major piece of luck for me to get to know him personally, I might easily not have. He influenced me greatly. "Oscar," he said to me at the time, "architecture is imagination – invention and imagination." That still impresses me. But stylistically I moved away from Le Corbusier even with my very first project. I found his architecture too heavy. He was devoted to right angles. I wanted to come up with a light architecture with more curves, and was fascinated by what reinforced concrete could do. That was the time when spanning wide spaces with concrete came in. Fantastic, I still get excited by it.

At the time, were the Europeans and Bauhaus modernism things you deliberately decided to steer clear of?

In my case, that was more a matter of intuition. Most Europeans built too functionally for my taste, so terribly monotonously and uniform. We can't be tied down by function, we aren't its slaves. Le Corbusier once said that the Bauhaus was a paradise of mediocrity. I wanted things to be bigger, more extensive and certainly not mediocre. If you like, you could say I was looking for a different way to go.

Where did you get the courage to go your own way like that?

Well, Corbusier was an artist, he thought of nothing else but architecture. And that didn't seem to me to be enough, which is why in the end someone else made much more of an impression on me, a Brazilian who wasn't an architect. That was lawyer Rodrigo Melo Franco de Andrade. He taught me that you always have to see architecture as a part of a whole, and he showed me the roots of Brazilian architecture. I also learnt from him how important it is for an architect to look around and read a lot.

You mean, so architecture doesn't become an end in itself.

Yes, precisely. That really would be terrible.

But what can architecture actually achieve, what power does it have?

I have to say, in that respect I'm pessimistic. Architecture doesn't change anything at all. If society is bad like here in Brazil, for example, even the best architect can accomplish nothing. In fact, I have my doubts whether people *can* be changed to the good. Really, life is just one big lottery, we're born white or black, stupid or bright – it's a genetic tombola. You see, a human being is like a house you can repaint, and you can move the walls, even, but if the original structure was badly designed and badly constructed, that's how it stays. There's virtually nothing you can do.

So if architecture can't make the New Man, what can it do? Is it just a question of the right style?

Style never interested me, and wasn't something I ever wanted to create. Nor do I see my buildings as models to be imitated all over the place. I don't have any recipes or general solutions off pat. Every architect should build the way he likes. For me, the important thing is to stick to my intuition. Do you follow? I have more than thirty books that are about my architecture, but I've preferred not to read them. I don't in the least want to know what they think of my buildings. The main thing is, *I* know. An ideal architecture accepted by everyone doesn't exist anyway. And it really would be very boring.

And how do you counter this boredom?

The important thing for me was always, there should be something surprising about my buildings. I wanted to come up with something that hadn't existed like that before, something no one had ever thought of previously. The buildings ought to overwhelm people with their beauty, they'd be so wonderful they'd gladden everyone's heart. Sometimes that might be a moment of happiness, even for the poor.

You've done your bit for the poor time and again, and you're still in the Communist Party. So why have you nonetheless worked for dictators and "class enemies"?

Oh come on, architects build for governments and also rich people.

At least you could also have built for the poorer population, for example, to improve things in the favelas.

You mean I should have fobbed off the poor with a handout or two, a few cheap shacks just to keep them quiet? I don't get involved in projects like that. Anyway, the social question can't be solved within the capitalistic system, whether democratic or not. Where does that leave me as an architect? I can build something everyone can enjoy, regardless of whether they are rich or poor. True, that's not much. But I never claimed otherwise.

Museum for Contemporary Art, Niterói, Rio de Janeiro, 1999

And what about your Communist ideals?
They are still important to me, but certainly. I still meet up with a few friends every Tuesday, and we discuss the latest political developments, in this country and abroad as well. Sometimes we organise protests or go on demonstrations if we don't like something. We also help people who have nothing and are being exploited.

But your architecture is also thoroughly political. At any rate, it's had a strong influence on the national identity, and the image of Brazil.
Could be, yes, my architecture is extremely specific. But I didn't invent it out of thin air. There are, I'd say, a few connections there, with the Baroque period and the landscape, of course. Le Corbusier once said to me, you have the mountains of Rio in your eyes. But it's more than the mountains, it's the women, it's the sky, the clouds, everything that's important. Curves have always fascinated me, the tension in them, the freedom. I wanted a lighter and a freer architecture. You know what I mean: with real enthusiasm.

And Brasilia, the new capital, then became the great experimental lab for this freedom?
When we started on Brasilia, I could do anything I wanted. It was a dream, albeit a very strenuous one. The city had to be finished in only four years, the president said – no one can imagine that these days. At that time, the whole country was full of optimism, that we were doing something that no one else was doing. The city was to be our utopia. There were to be no slums in it like in other metropolises, there'd be equality at last. The rich would live next to the poor, ministers alongside workers. When the city opened for business, that soon proved false, a delusion. The money barons came out on top, just as always.

But for a while you believed in the new start?
Yes, that was the idea. And for a time it seemed it might become reality. I remember we were driving to Brasilia, or rather to where Brasilia would one day be. And we ran into endless queues of cars, all of them construction workers from every part of the country, wanting to join in the building. They thought they'd find work and a happy life in Brasilia.

And you were expected to manage all those people?
I was at least expected to do the designs so that they could be built in such a short time in the first place. Well, to cope with that, I decided to emphasise first and foremost the structure of the buildings. The details were not so important, what mattered was the load-bearing frame. The technique decided the architecture and, as I said, reinforced concrete enabled me to do everything differently, more beautifully and variedly.

In other words, you went for the shape, the external appearance...

What else? You've no idea what it was like then. Normally there's a programme when you're constructing a new building, and in the case of a capital, particularly so. You know how many rooms, how many streets, how many offices and so on you have to build. We knew nothing at all, there was no programme. And we didn't have time to work one out. So we looked at the buildings of the old capital, Rio, and did that to the power of 10. The new technology made it possible, especially the concrete.

Where did your fascination with the material come from?

I was always keen to show progress in civil engineering techniques as well, and it worked in Brasilia. When the military dictatorship took over and I had to go to Europe, I soon discovered it was, for example, much more difficult to get my designs approved in France. The authorities generally wanted thicker walls than I would build them – in France they wanted 1.50 metres where I could it with 30 centimetres, the way I'd intended it. In Europe people tend to have second thoughts, whereas we have audacity, it seems to me. And that's also typical of a country that is so young and wants to show the world all the things it can do. At least, it was always important to me to conquer great spaces – not the columns, or the ceiling, it was the clear space between that fascinated me.

Meantime you've infected very many architects with this fascination – Frank Gehry for example. How do you like his buildings?

Yes, I do like them. But he builds much too lavishly and with such expensive materials. We couldn't afford that here at all. I've always gone for simple, clear shapes. If you can't draw architecture in a few strokes, then something is wrong. Only shapes you can easily take in offer the character, the uniqueness and memorability that is fast disappearing from cities the world over. They are all losing their individual, unified look.

Does that apply to Brasilia as well?

Yes, even there everything is being built more and more uniformly, especially on the edges of the city. Atrocious buildings they are, and then all the cars everywhere.

Don't you like Brasilia?

I like Rio. In Brasilia you go out of the hotel into the street, and then rush back into the hotel. If I could plan Brasilia all over again, I'd build the National Congress and Praça dos Três Poderes exactly as they are. Only there'd be extra apartment buildings and schools and shops. And I'd do without all the wide streets with all the cars. People would be able to walk everywhere.

You have, in fact, gone on designing new buildings for Brasilia, a museum, for example, which like many others of your buildings looks like a temple, a place of homage. When one sees your architecture, one could get the impression you are a religious person, a believer. I'd like to be religious. But mankind is too screwed up for me to believe in God. And you know, I don't believe in anything that promises eternity. Life is a breath, a minute, and then it's gone.

Is there still something that you want from life?
I'd like to stop talking about architecture. I'd prefer to talk about literature, women and science. If I were allowed a wish, then it's for everyone to be equally prosperous, please. For everyone to be happy. At present, the world seems to me terribly set. There's dissatisfaction everywhere, many people don't believe in the future, money reigns supreme. Even for that reason alone, architecture can't be the answer. Architecture isn't important, the world is important, and we have to change it. It's a shitty world.

The Congress buildings, Brasilia, 1957

FREI OTTO

MY PASSION IS FOR LIGHTNESS AND MOBILITY

They still want his advice, and call on him in the hills outside Stuttgart. Frei Otto, born 1925, is an architect, but not just that. He is an inventor, scholar, materials expert, and one of the most import-ant master builders of the twentieth century. Whenever things get a little tricky somewhere – if, for example, an architect such as Shigeru Ban wants to build a pavilion out of paper struts, he turns to Frei Otto, the freethinker. They are all welcome to his house in Leonburg. His house looks half laboratory, half hobby room. All his life he has seen himself as pure researcher, which is why he also founded the internationally highly regarded Institut für Leichte Flächentragwerke (Institute for Membrane Structures). Even now, his workshop is piled high with models made of plaster and pasteboard and women's stockings, with which he cobbles together his soaring roofs and screens. He was born in Chemnitz, and long wanted to be a stonemason or sculptor; but then he discovered flying, became fascinated by the exhilaration of being airborne, in World War II as well, when he was a fighter pilot. All his life, he has had a passion for provisional structures and temporary architecture. And this also means that many of his buildings have long since disappeared, such as his pavilion for the Expo in Montreal in 1967. Other buildings, like the roofs for the Olympic Stadium in Munich, have etched themselves deeply in the collective memory.

Herr Otto, are you someone who prefers to look forward – or back?
Looking is a bit of a thing for me. You see, my eyesight has become very bad, I'm almost blind. More than ever, my experience is that buildings evolve mainly in the head, and that as an architect you have to see them in your mind's eye and wander through them internally before they are built. Otherwise they're buildings that have only been calculated but never felt. Many colleagues pay too much attention to appearances, visual attractions, forgetting how important the inner values of a building are. Even if it sounds rather odd, ever since I've scarcely been able to make anything out any more, I see things in architecture much more clearly.

What do you see?
I see that it's worthwhile if you're old-fashioned like me and hold on to your hopes. There's no reason at all for this terrible gloom many people put on. We could be happy, we live in a time of change. There's no obligatory style you have to defer to. And that offers younger architects in particular the freedom to do what they really want. Yes, they do have to be clear about wanting. However, they need to look for the clarity in their minds, because computers, which many people are glued to, contain only what someone has put in them.

Amazing numbers of the younger architects think very highly of your architecture, your tent structures, most of all, of course, the floating roofs of the Olympic Stadium in Munich. Many people look up to you as a model. Does that amaze you?
I'm pleased, of course. The grandchildren seem to be approaching their grandparents with frankness and curiosity. Many people notice that computers have their limits. I've nothing against them, but my experience with materials and forms I can touch has taken me a good deal further. Some of the young ones are now discovering this treasury of experience. They're mostly from abroad, and come here to visit me in my secluded studio. There's less demand from Germans.

It was always the case that abroad you were considered a world architect and here you were often dismissed as an oddball and outsider. Do you mind the lack of respect?
Sometimes I do mind. I get far greater acknowledgment especially in Japan, but also in the USA and England. The Germans are sceptical if someone comes up with something new and unusual. They desperately look for tradition, and because they're uncertain about where they're coming from, they don't have enough assurance to get involved in experimentation. That's why German architects – even the younger ones – lack daring as well.

That would probably require a society that wanted different architecture. What are experiments for if they're not tied into a social project?
There you're making things too easy for yourself. There are truly enough unsolved tasks, and architects could put forward proposals. Architects are really needed for disaster protection, for example. Or just have a look at our cities. We can't go any further with the usual repertoire architects come up with; that's out of date. Especially with the

Shigeru Ban with Frei Otto, Japanese pavilion, Expo, Hanover, 2000

street grids that antiquity has landed us with – you can't build living cities with them. It's high time to try out something new.

What would you suggest?
Why not have a city centre full of high-density one-family houses again? Why not make it possible to have an urban life with greenery? That could be a challenge for young architects. But hardly anyone seems interested in that. Who's still experimenting?

There are a number of experiments, a lot of them especially trying out crazy structural shapes. But if I understand you rightly, what you're talking about is social experiments.
I'm talking about greater depth. We used to ask ourselves what architecture actually is. Or how we'll be living in the future. These days people ask what architecture looks

like. It infuriates me! It's not a matter of exteriors. People don't just have eyes, they have a great variety of far-reaching needs. That's why architects shouldn't be so terribly shallow in the questions they ask.

So they should be social scientists rather than designers?
Why not? A good architect is always a social worker and a family doctor, someone who doesn't prescribe what buildings people should have but helps them to build themselves suitable accommodation. There's a great willingness for people to try out new forms of self-build, many people enjoying designing them. Not architects though. Many of them secretly despise home-owners and make fun of their supposed petty bourgeois ways. They could try telling people what's possible. Very few people know about the huge range of possibilities. That's the only reason why people go for the well-tried approach and the clichés of prefabricated building manufacturers.

Are architects afraid of losing their sovereignty as designers?
Obviously. Many of them prefer to stick to the usual thing. It would need effort to ask about real needs. That lethargy is an opportunity for younger architects. They could invent mobile cities, accommodation for modern gypsies, diplomats, managers, anyone who's always on the move. For people like that, they could develop houses you can take with you or properly insulated tents. That may sound absurd, but you'll see, in 50 years' time mobile homes will be taken for granted.

Isn't the opposite true? Isn't the need for solid walls, unalterable structures growing, precisely because people's lives are more and more flexible?
You're right about that, the need for a secure foothold is growing. But I wonder whether mobility can be designed so it's home as well. Why shouldn't it be possible to resolve this contradiction?

Perhaps because many people feel flexibility is a threat, and so long for fixed tracks.
I don't want to prescribe to anyone where and how he should live. I'd never make an ideology out of my preferences. Eero Saarinen once said that every task has its particular solution. I like that. Architecture is a primeval technology, perhaps the oldest there is alongside weapons technology. And there's scarcely an invention in building that's considered finished with. There's a place for everything. Still, I have my passion, of course, which is for lightness and mobility.

Where did that passion come from?
It probably goes back to my early experiences as an architect. I did my last year at school in 1943, then I was called up and eventually finished up as a prisoner of war in France, in a camp that with 40,000 people was really a city. I got into the construction group, and suddenly found myself in charge of it, having to plan this mobile city, get hold of tents and adapt warehouses. We had virtually no materials, and built with practically nothing. I kept this nothing when I set up as an independent architect in 1952. We designed temporary things. I didn't mind, quite the contrary. After the

Nazis' mutterings about eternity, this nothing represented to me an opportunity to go down new roads. Simple and temporary became my leitmotif.

Was there a social aspiration involved in this art of making do?
Secretly, I did sense there was. I never went hawking it around, but my dream was that light, flexible buildings might lead to a new, open society. I've never been interested in eternity, and the fact that five of the thirteen buildings I've been able to build myself are now listed buildings is a bit of nuisance, really. It was always the moment that mattered to me, which is why, for example, we produced a building that lasted only three hours after we'd worked on it for six months. That was a marquee for the Berlin Philharmonic, when they played in front of Schloss Bellevue for the opening of Interbau. For three wonderful hours I was as happy as an architect can ever be.

German pavilion at the Montreal Expo, 1967

This confidence has sustained you all your life.
Well, of course, what sort of an architect doesn't have an appetite for the future? As designers, architects are always dealing with something that isn't there yet. They're asked to add something to the present that happens to be the future. Why should I be despondent? I was always firmly convinced that technology, research and innovation would take us somewhere. And I'm still right, we're doing uncommonly well. It's like living in Paradise.

Which Paradise do you mean?
Well, just look around. A building like this is just as Biblical tradition says. The temperature's between 19 and 28 degrees, we always have running water, flowers in the rooms, we don't really need any clothes.

Paradise also means innocence. Do your buildings express a longing to be rid of sin?
Inside me, yes, probably there is such a longing. But I've never said it aloud like that. I'm not a visionary, more of an inquiring mind who's interested in specific solutions, and structures.

But you've never been miserly with your feelings. You have a reputation for temper.
Yes, I probably do have a temper. Because temper is always an expression of a strong will.

Do we need more temper?
I'd be glad to see more temper particularly from the younger set, definitely.

I.M. PEI

I'D LIKE TO BE A SCULPTOR

You can easily misjudge Ieoh Ming Pei. A quiet, slightly built man, he's so unassuming you could easily fail to notice him. Yet for all his courteousness and friendly reticence, Pei always knew pretty precisely what he wanted, and he had the tenacity to win through. He was born in Canton [Guangzhou] in 1917, later moving with his family to Shanghai, where he was so impressed by the high-rise buildings that he decided to become an architect. Not just anywhere, but in the place where high-rise meant skyscrapers – the USA. He studied first at the MIT in Boston and then at Harvard, where he became an assistant to Bauhaus founder Walter Gropius. He won his first important contract – for the Kennedy Library – shortly after he set up an independent practice. That's where he established his style of large, clear shapes that won him many other projects – the extension of the National Gallery in Washington, the new building for the Bank of China in Hong Kong and finally the Louvre extension with its now celebrated glass pyramid. In Berlin, he was commissioned directly by the German Federal Chancellor Helmut Kohl to provide an extension for the German Historical Museum, and even there, in a very confined space, he came up with a tour de force of solidity and strength that seems quite out of keeping with his restful appearance.

What does a building have to be like for you to be happy with it?
Happy? You know, I always give my best shot, but I'm never satisfied. Of the 60 or so buildings I've been privileged to build during my life, I'm really happy with only a handful. You can always do things better.

Does that also apply to your most recent buildings, like the extension to the German Historical Museum in Berlin? Many people don't like the stair tower of your museum.
Yes, many people think it's a bit brash. But it's supposed to be, it's supposed to hit you in the eye. All architects like their buildings to be looked at. But in this case it's not just about my ego, it's about the building. It's overshadowed by Schinkel's Neue Wache and hidden behind Schlüter's massive Arsenal, and needs to be flagged architecturally. It's small, but has to have a big effect.

Is that why it has such an extravagant atrium? It looks almost as if it were the entrance hall to a huge, important collection.
What's on show there is also important, and the architecture's intended to stress that. It's supposed to entice people to go round the whole building with great pleasure and curiosity. I want to attract them even up to the top floor, the fourth floor, with a succession of staircases and new views and panoramas. That's why what you call extravagant is in truth a ruse. The architecture is supposed to get people to forget all the effort that visiting a museum involves.

To get the interplay of vistas you wanted, you opened up the hall with glass façades. Wouldn't a stone façade have been more appropriate at this spot, in a site trapped between Schlüter and Schinkel buildings?
But I don't ignore history, I just write the next page.

Was Schinkel a formative influence?
To me, he is undoubtedly the most important German architect, more important than Mies van der Rohe.

One wouldn't know that from your building.
I'm not a historicist, I lack any talent for neoclassicism. But I do follow Schinkel's spirit completely. For example, his Neue Wache impresses me. It is small and compact, and was built of cheap, almost waste materials, and yet it's immensely impressive. It's modest in scale, yet monumental in effect. That's a principle not unknown in my building either. Schinkel had an enviable capacity to come up with intimacy and delicacy as much as the absolute.

But even so, you're not addicted to his forms.
We can learn a lot from architects of that time. But that doesn't mean I have to act as if I were living in the past.

German Historical Museum, Berlin, 2003

Hasn't your architectural idiom already long become history? It was developed in the twentieth century, in the modernist era that's now passé.

You're right. But modernism still means something to me. I live my forms. I don't imitate or copy them, but try to develop them further. My instinct is that these belong to our time.

But the Bauhaus is nearer to you than Schinkel.

No, there you're wrong. I did study with Walter Gropius, the former director of the Bauhaus, but I was never a disciple like many others. His theories never struck an inward chord, which is why I turned to Mies van der Rohe as well, once I'd graduated. That may sound obvious to you, that's how people do it nowadays, going from one thing to another. But it was different then. If Gropius had got wind I was going to Mies, he'd have been beside himself. You had to stick to a single school of thought.

But you never stuck to any school particularly.
That's true. I soon had enough even of Mies. And today it's actually only Le Corbusier I can still get excited about. I often met him and chewed the fat with him.

What was it in him that fascinated you?
Mainly the strength of his spaces, his capacity for plastic design. When you look at Gropius or his colleagues in comparison, everything with them is so rigorous and often relentlessly smooth. Their buildings are practical but unexciting. Though Gropius was, in fact, even freer than Mies. I've never seen anything more boring that Mies's buildings for the Illinois Institute of Technology. They consist of nothing but design, and formally they're frozen stiff. I'm driven by an urge to get away from tedious grids. And Corbusier was more relaxed in his buildings than all the others, more humanistic.

More humanistic?
Yes, his buildings have something very personal and vital about them. That impressed me with Marcel Breuer as well, whom I experienced like a brother. He could achieve things with architecture that were immediate and warming. In a Mies building you have to wear a tux, in Gropius a necktie, but with Breuer you can turn up in a T-shirt.

And what do we wear in your buildings?
I admit I don't have Breuer's warmth, they're probably too monumental for that. And that's a defect. Though, unlike me, Breuer had the chance to build lots of houses, which challenge you to build humanistically. I've only built one house – my own.

Why?
Because I only got commissions for banks and museums. And because to start with I worked for a property developer. My father was a banker, and recommended me there, thinking it was a safe thing. Of course, I learnt a lot about the political and business side of building. Even so, I had the feeling of making a deal with an enemy. Those were ten frustrating years, I couldn't build anything good, only huge housing estate projects. And even high-rise office blocks and museums are more impersonal than country villas.

Yet people describe museums as the cathedrals of our time.
That's a bit over the top. But in the case of the Louvre, it was my aim as well to build a structure that would rouse the eight million people who visit it every year. Something that would stir them, perhaps even provoke an opinion about it, for example, "Do you like this thing?" "No, I hate it."

That doesn't sound as if you were looking for mystic sublimity with your architecture.
There are architects who imbue their buildings with a spiritual charge and awaken quasi-religious feelings in individual visitors. I was more interested in the communal aspect. I never succeeded in getting the kind of thing that Louis Kahn, for example, achieved. But I didn't even want to.

Glass pyramid, Louvre, Paris, 1989

But Kahn did influence you very much with his massive structural corpuses, didn't he?
I was very impressed by his building in Philadelphia. Though it doesn't work as a
research centre, it's grand as architecture. I went specially to see Kahn at the time to say
how much I liked that building. All he said was, go to Scotland and look at the castles.
That impressed me even more.

You mean wild and timeless?
No architect wants his buildings to be torn down after twenty-five years. He wants
them to last. His ego expects it. So he has to design a building that is liked and is
important. Too important just to disappear.

Building for eternity.
Yes. Though I've already lost an office block, and what's more, it was Philip Johnson
who destroyed it. It was my first and not especially good. Even so, it was a pity.

To create something durable – was that why you decided to become an architect?
Oh, at that time I was very naïve. I'd spent some years in Shanghai in the twenties,
when the city was growing at breakneck speed like now. I was impressed you could
construct 23-storey buildings. I wanted to do the same, and went to America to study.

Did that mean forgetting China?

Yes, or at least the forms and styles were no longer relevant. But to me China has never totally disappeared. I've been living in America for 68 years now, and yet still feel Chinese. Isn't that odd? I got myself a new skin, but inside everything was already there. And whenever I hear something about China, it always affects me deeply.

Do your origins determine your architecture?

If only I knew. Sometimes I feel inspired by the traditions of Chinese calligraphy, sometimes by a Western artist such as Anselm Kiefer, whom I consider one of the greatest painters.

Are artists trailblazers for you?

They're my cousins, at any rate.

Would you like to be an artist?

Yes, I'd like to be a sculptor. I envy them their freedom, the way they can shape space. Make something transcendent out of it.

There are architects who allow themselves this freedom.

Frank Gehry, for example. But in his case the shape always comes first, and the space is only a secondary product. But the two should relate to one another. I admire Frank, but I prefer rigorous, clear forms, even in art. To me, Malevich, for example, or Barnett Newman have great formative power. It's all there in their works, they bring out the essentials.

What about music? Does that also affect your buildings?

Unfortunately, I lack the talent to be a musician. But my mother was a flautist, and even now I'm always listening to music, even when working. It fills and opens up spaces. It lives from movement, and never stands still. To me, it's just the same with good architecture. You can experience it only if you move through it, if you see it as something open you keep going back to. You must know Balthasar Neumann's pilgrimage church of Vierzehnheiligen, a Baroque miracle. I've been there three times, inside that place. It's immensely sensual, very exciting. To me, Vierzehnheiligen is music.

In truth, you're a Baroque architect.

Well, southern Italian Baroque churches don't impress me at all, there's nothing delicate and soaring about them. That's like in Rome, St Peter's, everything is geared towards a single objective. It's a church that aims at shock and awe, and tries to force you on to your knees. Whereas Vierzehnheiligen is full of mystery and doesn't come at you. It has thousands of ways to it, ways of looking at it. I try to get something of that kind across in my buildings, for example, the National Gallery in Washington, D.C.

Though that doesn't look completely liberated.

No, I'm an architect of squares and triangles, not a computer architect. Where Neumann could lick everything into shape with plaster and mortar, I have to think how to produce the whole thing in an industrial age. Divergences are important, but very expensive. Unless you program it all on computer. If I were starting out now, things would be easier.

Does age make for work?
A lot of things take more time, I get tired more quickly. And I have to watch out that I don't turn out too much nonsense. Many late works by other architects are disastrous. That's another reason I don't do much any more. And if I accept a job, then it's only to fulfil myself. In old age, you have to be very egotistical.

How do you mean?
If, for example, I build the Museum of Islamic Art in Qatar, I tell myself, now's your opportunity to learn something about Islam at last, from Mahomet to the Ottoman Empire. Though I'm old, I'm still healthy and can still poke around. I want to catch up on things I've missed out on. Our time offers me all kinds of opportunities to do that.

Was the twentieth century a good century for architects?
It was for me. When has it ever been possible for one architect to learn so much and build in so many different places? When was it possible for a Chinese to go to America and then subsequently design buildings for Europe? Or for Asia, where now, at the end of my life, I'm building a museum, in my home town. They've been asking for ten years whether I'd design it. Now's probably the time to do it.

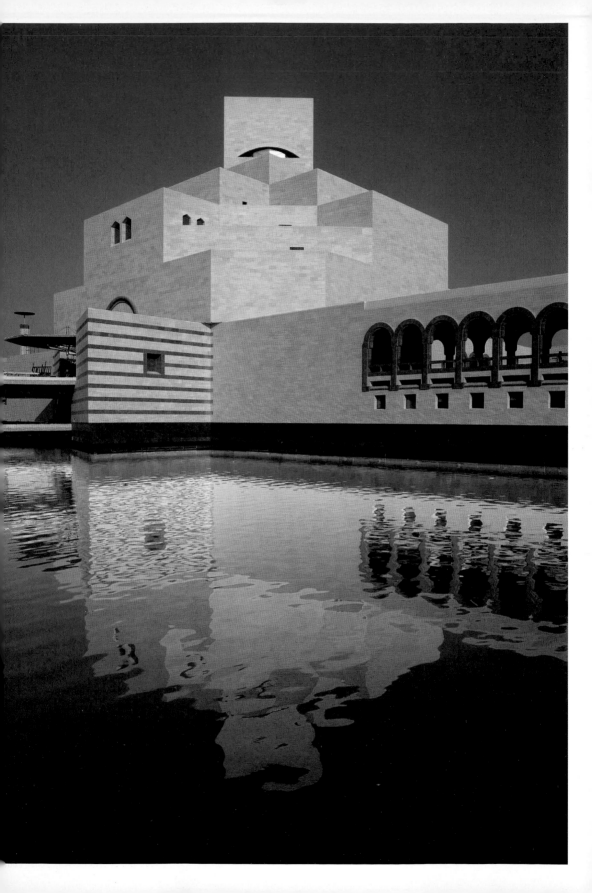

ROBERT VENTURI & DENISE SCOTT BROWN

PEOPLE HAVE A RIGHT TO BEAUTIFUL ARCHITECTURE

Architects don't look like this, not like these two, who look as if they'd spent their whole lives in a small university in Kansas, perhaps as professors of English literature. And yet Robert Venturi and Denise Scott Brown are among the most combative of architectural theorists of the present day. Their book Learning from Las Vegas, *first published in 1972 , has long been a classic. Likewise,* Complexity and Contradiction in Architecture *of 1966 has been printed and reprinted and translated into many languages. They have also built widely, the Sainsbury Wing of the National Gallery in London, for example, where they endeavoured to update neoclassicism. Venturi (born 1925) and his wife Scott Brown (born 1931) still run their office in Philadelphia. However, despite such grand cultural projects they specialise, as well, in the mundane and everyday and see architecture as something that should respond to the many tastes of a multicultural society. Many critics denigrate them as postmodernists because of their populist idiom. But that doesn't bother them much. They dismiss the criticism with a shrug and a knowing smile. Just as wise professors would do.*

Ms Scott Brown, Mr Venturi, your books are standard reading for all architectural students, and many of your colleagues have been inspired by your research into Las Vegas. Yet there's scarcely an architectural firm that is more despised than yours. Why?

RV: Many people think we're arch-enemies of modernism. That's nonsense, of course. We love architects such as Alvar Aalto, and hats off to Le Corbusier's Villa Savoye. Though we allow ourselves to observe that this modernism has long since become history, just like the Renaissance and the Baroque. So it's about time to be on the lookout for twenty-first-century architecture. Yet most of our colleagues don't want to admit it.

DSB: Sometimes it seems to me as if the Russian Constructivists were still alive. They thought that, come the Revolution, the masses would fall into line with their way of doing things. Likewise, many architects think they can force their taste on the whole world – that everyone should pick up the ideas of the upper middle classes.

You mean there's a kind of dictatorship of taste? Isn't architecture today more varied than ever before?

DSB: That's as may be, but what the masses like is still considered vulgar. Architects have retreated into the ghetto of high aesthetics. And they fight against everything that contradicts their notions of design, however heterogeneous those may be. And then they also grumble that they've been sidelined these days.

RV: Denise is right. There's no denying that the idea of an International Style continues to be prevalent. People believe in architecture that is supposed to be equally suitable anywhere for any purpose. Behind it, there's the notion that there's only one culture that can unite people, the right one. Like 80 years ago, everything's still supposed to be new and revolutionary today as well – you're not allowed to believe in evolutionary architectural history. But then both can be justified: sometimes it's time for revolutions, sometimes you have to be able to be tradition-minded. There's no other way if you want to do justice to a multicultural society.

DSB: Architects talk about the human dimension of architecture, as if there's only one dimension that's human. Rather unworldly, isn't it?

And you think it's because of this that many people are not interested in architecture?

RV: For most people, modern architecture is much too abstract. They want vitality that's more ordinary, that's not so difficult to understand.

DSB: Good architecture doesn't have to be so out of touch. It needn't be dreamed up by crazy geniuses, it can be designed by good craftspeople and accessible to everyone.

RV: Many architects act as if we were still living in the industrial age and had to build offices made of steel and glass that look like factories. What we ourselves do is try to make use of the advertising and entertainment industries as sources of ideas. It doesn't seem to us appropriate any more to pursue architecture into abstraction and keep on reducing and reducing it. That was an important development early last century, but these days it needs to be about opening up architecture to meaning again and giving it new symbolic force.

Vanna Venturi House, Chestnut Hill, Philadelphia, 1964

But classic modernism wasn't that abstract. Many symbolic buildings were built at that time, think, for example, of the steamer motifs of Eric Mendelsohn.
RV: I agree with you there. But the avant-garde never admitted they were working on meaning. Even today, symbolism and narrative are mostly despised.
DSB: Though many architects build symbols, they are usually symbols meaningful to them and a few colleagues. But such forms of self-realisation can't be all that it's about. Architects are not the divinities that the genius-obsessed nineteenth century wanted to make them. They have to serve society and their clients. Which doesn't mean that they have to be dependent solely on their clients. Indeed, they need to formulate their design tasks more broadly than they do. And their buildings can communicate a much broader array of information.

Does that also mean architecture needs to strive for more beauty?
RV: Not at all. The meaning of a building is much more important than the expression and shape of a building. We tend to use the word meaning only when we're talking about literature, but that's wrong. Architecture should also say something to us again, just as churches once did. After all, they didn't just stand there mutely, they were buildings of immense eloquence.

At that time, there was a much more coherent outlook. Architects of the present can't draw on things like that.
DSB: They could at least try to discover new coherences. And perhaps they might succeed if they allowed ornamentation again. If you look back in architectural history, there were always decorative elements that told you a lot about the client and the era.

Our buildings today are mostly silent, they're dumb – and so they're not loved.
RV: Many architects are intoxicated with their belief in sincerity, in honest buildings that are only what they pretend to be. But there's also honest ornament, building decoration that's employed quite deliberately to give the building meaning. What's hypocritical about that?

That sounds as if you're advocating a witty postmodernism full of historical borrowings.
DSB: Come on, now. We've never gone in for reproducing history, allusions – little touches – were all. That's why we see postmodernism as a colossal misunderstanding.
RV: We dream of multicultural diversity. We want to mix history with the present, and we're not particularly keen on the distinction between high culture and pop culture, either. We like the ordinary and the ugly. And perhaps this preference is infectious – there are now hats on sale in the art museum in our home city, Philadelphia, with *ordinary* and *ugly* written on them. That's a kind of watchword for our firm.

Why's that? Do you want to continue the numerous uglinesses of the present day into the future?
DSB: Not at all. We're not anxious to design repulsive buildings. But you can learn a lot from ordinariness, much more than if you're always aiming for something that's heroic and original. If everything were always extraordinary, what kind of crazy/boring world would we be living in then?
RV: There's a long tradition of art that observes ordinariness and gets ideas from it.
DSB: There's Pop Art. Pop Art met ordinariness with sympathy, it brought tomato soup cans and comic characters into the museums. But it changed them, exaggerated their scale and swapped their contexts. Yes, we learned a lot from Pop Art.

Are there artists today you learn things from?
RV: Jenny Holzer, perhaps. Though her works seem a bit too polite to me, they don't have anything of the beautiful, vital vulgarity of non-commercial art. She's too pure for us. We're for impurity.
DSB: That's why we set off for Las Vegas in the 1960s – to find out the patterns the architecture followed there, the effects the architecture had, how it was used. We were thrilled by those buildings, they weren't pussyfooting around dreaming of a better world, they were entirely committed to reality and its laws. Not necessarily to be subject to them, but to understand them – to understand people's yearnings and find an architectural response to them.
RV: Yes, that was one thing. The other was that our trip to Las Vegas was probably to emancipate ourselves from the dogmas of modernism.
DSB: And to learn about the emerging form of the automobile city.

At least with your buildings you haven't yielded to the obsession with spectacle.
RV: For us, architecture is above all an art in the background. At least it's in good hands there, it doesn't have to keep pushing itself forward. But there are exceptions, where it can be crazy and egotistical, in Times Square, for example, in the centre of New York.

Are architects so much their own masters that they can choose where and what they design? Doesn't the client decide about spectacle or reticence?

DSB: Market forces are more powerful than architects or clients. They govern the forms of the city and often the appearance of buildings. No architect can wholly oppose these forces, but there are opportunities to get round them or make use of them to achieve your ideas.

RV: Your question is targeted at the ethics of our profession, and unfortunately that's a subject too rarely discussed. Many make things simple for themselves, by asserting that an architect can and should ride out the waves of reality. Yet, some aspects of reality can be changed with buildings. And if need be, an architect can always refuse a commission.

Have you ever done that?

RV: Yes, we have, for various reasons. One was a lucrative opportunity in the Middle East. We didn't feel comfortable with the social conditions in the country. We didn't want to make a deal with the rulers.

DSB: But the problem has other dimensions. Architects often talk about "humanity" and "the masses". Yet these terms are too broad. It would be better if they looked at smaller, better defined groups and at the opportunities their reality offered. The dividing line between arrogance and sticking to your principles is often not clearly recognisable. When do I man the barricades to fight my cause? When should I acknowledge that ideals of beauty vary greatly between social groups and therefore architecture can't always be the same, either?

If you have fights of this kind with yourselves and your clients, what actually are you struggling for? Or to put it differently: would our world really be worse if there were only bad architects?

DSB: I won't deny that you can live a nice life even in terrible architecture. It's often claimed that we build our buildings then our buildings make us, but I'm afraid that's just a fairy tale. Of course, a beautiful building can delight us and stimulate our senses, and it can often simplify and serve our lives. And architects have a moral responsibility not to make things worse, as they sometimes have done. But architecture doesn't make us better people.

RV: But it doesn't have to. Who's expecting it to? People have a right to beautiful architecture. Not for moral reasons, but because it can be a pleasure to look at it and live in it. And it's a pleasure that ought to be available to everyone.

Seattle Art Museum, 2005

PETER ZUMTHOR

BEING A COMPOSER IS SOMETHING I'D GO FOR

It's a sticky afternoon in August, with the sky overcast. We are sitting in the garden room, with the doors open wide and not a hint of a breeze. It gets darker and darker, a storm is brewing. And Peter Zumthor almost seems to disappear in the darkness, only his cigar glows. He lives out in the country in a place called Haldenstein, where he has built himself a wooden house, unadorned like everything he designs. Born in 1943, he originally wanted to make furniture, like his father, who taught him the trade. Then he worked in the preservation of historic monuments for some time, finally setting up as an architect in 1979. Most of his buildings are in Switzerland, like his thermal baths in Vals, for example. But his designs for the museum in Bregenz and the Kolumba Museum in Cologne made him an international name. Recently the controversy over the Topography of Terror memorial in Berlin has made him the stuff of legend. Zumthor's conscientiousness, also his awkward manner, make him both famous and feared wherever he works. Even as we start to talk, he just mutters, and only hesitantly begins to talk about himself. But then the conversation develops very well. And without us really noticing, it starts to rain outside.

When I read all the articles about you in recent years, I became a little apprehensive. You're described there as a monk, as an apostle, a shaman, mystic and guru. Are you a shining light, Herr Zumthor?
Well, you know, every day I get enquiries from students, colleges, magazines and possible clients, and because I turn a lot of things down so as to be able to work in peace, a kind of legend springs up. Many people seem to believe I'm a kind of Alpine hermit who does his work living in celibacy on bread and water and with no TV. What can I do about such myth-making? I can only watch in amazement.

There must be some reason for the enthusiasm, even so.
I do things all architects dream about. They're trained at college as architects, but in practice they just provide a service, they work just like caretakers or heating technicians. I resist that, because I build only what I want to. So unlike many colleagues, I'd never blame a bad building on the client or the building regulations. Because before I let myself be violated, I prefer to say no. All the defects you see in my buildings are my responsibility. That way, there are no excuses.

Is that the reason that many people are also afraid of you as an uncompromising fighter? In Berlin, the job was taken from you even though half of it, for the Topography of Terror, a museum about the Nazis, was already half-built. The accusation was made that costs were escalating.
But I didn't get my sums wrong. Many people in the building department told me we'd have to make a start on the building first, and the shortfall would be approved later. I was naïve, I admit.

What would have been special about that building?
To a layman I'd say, this house is to be built in a way you've never seen. A unique building for a unique spot. It wouldn't symbolise anything or illustrate anything, hence the reduction to pure structure, not a shape. It was an attempt at localisation. If you're doing a building that avoids all historical typologies, you've created a kind of semantic vacuum. The building is then just a symbol of itself, a symbol of the place where it stands.

Despite the vacuum, your building would nevertheless have sent a signal and in a way also aestheticised the crimes of the Nazi era.
You can't avoid a strong building also having an intellectual, metaphysical or semantic aura. But it shouldn't ossify into a threatening symbol. It should look beautiful, light and cheerful.

Say that again ... beautiful and cheerful?
Yes, definitely. You can't counter terrible things with horror. We don't need sombre event-architecture in order to remember, or understand, or be amazed. In the formidable monument that is Eisenman's stele memorial, I see the beginning of another catastrophe lurking within. The memorial seems to me immensely rigid. It tries to discipline people. Even in the memory, a military stance is adopted.

Kunsthaus Bregenz, 1997

And your building would have brought peace?
A building on a site directly associated with the catastrophe must be calm and peaceful, to allow memory and understanding to work. It has to pierce the didactic precondition-ing of the Holocaust phenomenon and put media magic behind it.

Many of your buildings embody self-containment and intactness. They should heal wounds, you once said.
But in Berlin, I wanted to keep the wound open. That's why I didn't want to build any-thing that was easily comprehensible or ticked boxes.

Isn't that true of almost all your buildings?
When I get a new building job, a new location, I go there and look round and in my mind begin to set out possible materials for possible anatomies. And I look to see what energies start to flow there.

Flowing energies?
When I'm designing – working – I mainly follow my inclination. It's a process of great naivety where everyone can have a say regardless of how much idea he has of architec-ture. The important thing is to be able to imagine things as a picture. Unfortunately, 80 per cent of architects can't imagine things three-dimensionally. For them, architec-ture is only a drawing on paper, and they don't translate that into an idea of what it will one day be.

So you proceed like a writer?
I listen to my inner ear and see what experiences I can call on to tackle a new building job. I often experience that – as writers say – the book writes itself. You make a start and then have to let go to find out where the material is taking you. I find it quite surprising how the images come up in my mind – sometimes it's like in the cinema. It's in moments like that where I'm not in control that the essence of the design emerges. But also as the design progresses, it occurs that I wake up and find myself somewhere in the building and think to myself, that wall or this door's not quite right. I don't have to do anything, it just comes.

Sounds as if you compose buildings rather than design them. Could your architecture be translated into music?
It might sound like Luigi Nono. Or Aaron Copland. Or even Heinz Holliger. But mainly I sense similarities with contemporary compositions where you have to listen the same way you look at a picture, i.e., they work with density, space, movement and tonal colour. Being a composer is something I'd go for. Perhaps in my next life.

What instruments would you write music for, then?
Luciano Berio wrote a collection of pieces in which he provided a solo piece for every single instrument, with the aim of bringing out the actual quality of that instrument. I like that very much, of course, because I'd also like to get my materials sounding that way. So I'd probably also get an oboe playing something that only the oboe can play. Which is really an oboe then.

If you're so keen on music, why are you still an architect?
The nice thing about architecture is that you're always building for a use you can measure ideas against. You can ask, now is it nice to be sitting here in the bath at nine and relaxing? Or is there anything that irritates me, perhaps the light's not right, or maybe I knocked my elbow. You can check against the function whether things work the way they should. And in the end that's the most important thing.

So the ideas you sketch out are soft and diffuse. Why are your buildings so austere and abstract?
Though the forms are hard and abstract, the atmosphere would have to be soft. As objects, the buildings often have something hard about them before they grow into themselves over time. Even a touch of pride and self-assurance. They tend to be free-standing, and create a presence in the locality. Often they're a declaration of love to the landscape. But on the inside, my buildings have a warm quality. Inside and outside is not the same in my case. You're never exposed, you have the wall behind you.

Then architecture is more maternal than paternal?
Always something maternal. Always sheltering, never didactic. More receptive and facilitating.

Does this mean you're setting yourself against classic modernism, which dreamt of openness and intangibility?

The idea of openness, the notion that everything is connected with everything fascinates me as well. But when I see what outstanding colleagues such as Rem Koolhaas make of these ideas, I preferred the ideas. His buildings aren't well made, I can scarcely see into the corners. It annoys me to see how badly the buildings age, how badly they're finished. But what mainly disturbs me about such buildings is the showing off. I don't like architecture making people look silly and encouraging them to make fools of themselves.

What was your objection?

My idea of architecture is always very physical. I like materials that wear, keep and have resonance. A few weeks ago I heard Andreas Staier, one of the best fortepiano players in the world, being asked why he liked playing Schubert. With Schubert, he said, there's no showing off and there's always intimacy. Then I thought, aha, so there are others who think the way I do. Of course, showiness is needed now and then, it's also a legitimate feature in urban development, but my passion is for intimacy. And for me, that means directness.

But also retreat. For example, your museum in Bregenz shuts itself up behind panes of matt glass, so that visitors don't get a look at Lake Constance. Why so introverted?

The way I imagine a museum is like this. I believe in the spiritual values of art, and have myself experienced that works of art can promote transcendence. They intimate to us that we are incorporated in something greater that we don't understand. I'm fascinated by this non-rational, mental or spiritual element, such as appears most clearly in early German Romanticism, for example, by Novalis or Caspar David Friedrich.

Heidegger as well?

I don't know much of his work, but when I read his texts where the ideas come thick and fast, then I get a sense of what he was looking for. I can understand his yearning for the primeval source, the safe billet and being at home.

Are your buildings resistance structures?

Yes, they oppose the increasing division of labour in construction. I don't want to be just a designer or at best a philosopher, which is why my buildings proclaim that it is not just images and ideas that govern our world. There are things as well, and these have an intrinsic value.

A longing for a permanent foothold is something many people feel, and not infrequently they want historicist architecture that looks as if it had always existed. Your buildings run contrary to such nostalgia. Why?

Both always existed – the need for reformulation and the need to be part of a tradition. I'm quite comfortable with that, I take over things at times that already existed. Nonetheless, I feel a great pleasure if I can say, I haven't copied anything, what I've produced is my own.

Thermal baths, Vals, 1996

Kolumba Museum, Cologne, 2007

You've said a lot now about your experiences and a lot about your feelings. Doesn't the subject of society play any part?
At any rate, I've said goodbye to the overworked notion that architecture has to save the world. What a building has to offer is very modest.

Is that a 1968 convert I'm listening to?
I was indeed one of the 1968 generation, though rather tepidly, and got involved in historical monuments because architecture was at the time politically a rather discreditable profession. Seen in retrospect, the whole movement seems to me culturally rather sectarian. Artists tried to inflate their importance by getting involved in politics, social affairs and economics. As they chased around after one theory or another, the aesthetic side got sidetracked, and art vanished. I was never more alienated than I was then.

Have you overcome this alienation today?
These days I think very closely about what I do and don't do. I can see no point in building a third or fourth villa for Hugo Boss, a catwalk for Armani or a hotel for Ian Schrager in New York, so I turned these enquiries down. Often, in such cases it's only a question of commerce – the generation of images and advertising. On the other hand, right here in the next valley we're doing a wooden house for a family with six children, on which our firm has already spent 60,000 Swiss francs. We did a chapel for a farming family in the Eifel, that was also virtually for nothing, charging only for expenses. So I do look at what I do and don't do.

But there are architects who take on more than the odd building or so and get involved in large-scale radical social changes. Why don't you?
Yes, I know. Rem Koolhaas, for example. He embraces present-day culture, and that in itself impresses me – not going against the current, not wanting to improve mankind but accepting what is. Nor do I want to tie anyone to my apron strings.

But what kind of influence do you have, then? Don't you mind that 98 per cent of all single-family houses are built by prefabricated firms – and architects simply stand by and watch?
I don't mind, not any more. Wailing about that sort of thing is pointless. I prefer to limit myself to individual locations, in the hope that these will have some effect, perhaps

like an acupuncturist's needle. In any case, I just can't handle a lot of things. I have an office with fourteen people, not 40 or 140 – and that's how it will remain, because I want to work the way I want. Because I want to know the door handles in every building. I'm not like Behnisch, who told me ten years ago that when he was carrying out his designs he looked only at the roof and the façade, the rest was done by his talented young architects. That's an attitude I respect, and that's how most of my colleagues work. But I don't.

To me, that sounds as if you built your buildings always for yourself.
For me, everything begins with spaces and objects that I love. And I can only do what I love. That's why there's nothing of the missionary in my buildings either, but just the young boy who's doing what he enjoys – and hopes that people will approve. And that they'll flatter me a little and say, you've done that nicely. It's that simple.

And when is a good building good?
For the people who use one of my buildings, it can be an incredible source of pleasure. My grandmother's house was like that.

Was that built by an architect?
No, it was a farmhouse.

Don't you need an architect for good architecture?
I don't care in the least who does it, it simply needs to be done. And I'm proof that it still works that way. That buildings can still be built that people remember with pleasure.

Is melancholy your greatest passion?
Together with intimacy and cheerfulness – yes, maybe.

Epilogue

There was no plan behind it, no grand scheme. But when you now reread the conversations that have appeared over the years in Die Zeit, you can easily get the impression that the architects concerned were talking not only to me as the interviewer but to each other. It is almost as if they were having a debate about the basic values of architecture. I have been Die Zeit's architectural critic since 1998, and whenever an important building or major exhibition opened, I often met the architects. Sometimes we fixed a time for an interview as well. They were conversations about immediate matters, but they have not dated. At least, it is my impression that they have retained their topicality.

When the architects read through their answers again for this book, there was virtually nothing they wanted to update. The conversations were clearly about the great whys and wherefores – just questions that lose nothing of their importance even in times of radical change. Indeed, the issues have become all the more pressing.

I would like to thank all the architects who were willing to spend a little time pondering and reflecting, and set aside time and leisure for the discussions. My equally sincere thanks to all those who have worked on this book in the background – Katharina Haderer, Curt Holtz, Paul Aston, my colleagues, my parents and my wife.

Hamburg, August 2008

Photo Credits

Iwan Baan: pp. 7, 13, 102
Cecil Balmond: pp. 20, 24
Behnisch Architekten: p. 28
Fabrizio Bergamo: p. 80
Petr Berka: p. 64
Marcus Bredt/gmp: p. 68
Buchheim Museum: p. 32
Wilfried Dechau/gmp: p. 66 left
Steve Double: p. 78
Todd Eberle: p. 58; Todd Eberle/Herzog & de Meuron: p. 82
Gerry Ebner: p. 150
Rollin La France/VSBA: p. 146
Foster + Partners: p. 52
Klaus Frahm/gmp: p. 73
Franz Marc Frei: p. 140
Christian Gahl/gmp: p. 70
Dominik Gigler: p. 96
Dennis Gilbert/VIEW: p. 27
gmp: p. 66 right
Florian Göcklhofer: p. 152
Jeff Goldberg/Esto: p. 43
Thomas Graham/Arup: p. 18
Roland Halbe/Artur: p. 132
Franz Hanswijk/VSBA: p. 144
Christian Heeb: pp. 9, 92
Jürgen Hohmuth: p. 39
Jaro Hollan: p. 8
Werner Huthmacher: p. 74
Ingenhoven Architekten: p. 134
"Introduction to Saadiyat Island Cultural
    District", Abu Dhabi, 2008: p. 10
Christian Kandzia: p. 136
Rainer Kiedrowski: p. 30
Studio Daniel Libeskind: p. 108
Heiner Leiska/gmp: p. 71
Greg Lynn: pp. 116, 119
Thomas Mayer: p. 63
Norman McGrath: p. 95
Rudi Meisel: p. 46
Museum of Islamic Art, Doha: p. 143
Stefan Müller: pp. 110, 113, 115
Cathleen Naundorf: p. 129
Office for Metropolitan Architecture: p. 99
Prada: p. 86
Eckhard Ribbeck: p. 122
Christian Richters: pp. 76, 155
Ulrich Schwarz: p. 138
Katsumasa Tanaka: p. 44
Ted Thai/Getty Images: p. 90
Matt Vargo/VSBA: p. 149
Elke Wetig: p. 156
Nigel Young/Foster + Partners: pp. 55, 57